Andre Holloway is a youth minister, culinary chef, youth basketball coach and now a newly published author. Although he is a novice writer with limited experience, he is experienced in telling his story through public speaking and as a mentor to young adults. Living and growing up in South Central LA in the '70s, he witnessed and experienced death, being shot and how drugs took a toll on his family, as well as his community. He also realized the importance of faith and family, and how that got him through the tragedies he experienced as a teen.

I like to dedicate this book to my parents, Trular Holloway and Autry Thomas Holloway Sr., who did their best to raise me up to be the man that I am today, through the good times and the bad. And also my parents in the Lord, overseer Dorothy Thompson, the woman of God and Pastor John Thompson, who are my in-laws as well. They both helped me to become the spiritual man that I am today. I can remember my mother-in-law, the woman of God praying for my deliverance on many occasions, tarrying with me all night long. All four of them greatly influence my life. A.L.H.S.

Andre Holloway

BUSTLE

The Tragedies and Triumphs of a Teen Growing up in Compton, Ca.

AUSTIN MACAULEY PUBLISHERS™

LONDON • CAMBRIDGE • NEW YORK • SHARJAH

Ordering Information
Quantity sales: Special discounts are available on quantity purchases by corporations, associations, and others. For details, contact the publisher at the address below.

Publisher's Cataloging-in-Publication data
Holloway, Andre
Bustle

ISBN 9781649798237 (Paperback)
ISBN 9781649798244 (ePub e-book)

Library of Congress Control Number: 2021914575

www.austinmacauley.com/us

First Published (2021)
Austin Macauley Publishers LLC
40 Wall Street, 33rd Floor, Suite 3302
New York, NY 10005
USA

mail-usa@austinmacauley.com
+1 (646) 5125767

I would like to thank my coworkers, who helped me throughout this journey of writing my book. The bus drivers: Kimberly Hernandez, Danielle Mitchell, and Conna Moreno. The school nurse Mrs. Sonya Perkins and her daughter. In the earlier stages of my book, Mrs. Perkins daughter helped me greatly with editing portions of my book, which set me in the right direction that I needed to go in to completing my book. Also Miss Johnson helped me with spelling and grammar. I appreciate you all so very much. Special thanks to my wife and children for giving me extreme helpful input. Much love to you all. A.L.H.S.

Table of Contents

This is a story about a young black man who grew up in Compton, California, who overcame the tragedy of being shot, not once but twice. And then all the difficulties that came after, while surviving the relentless '70s, all before the age of 18.

Introduction

This book is for anyone who wants a closer walk with the Lord. It doesn't matter who you are, where you were born, your skin complexion, your gender, or if you were born into riches or into poverty. You can still have a closer relationship with God.

Now this story just so happens to be talking about a young black teenager, who grew up in Compton California but don't let that deter you from reading this book. There are a lot of ups and downs in everyone's life, and this is the story of my life, my ups and downs, my friends, and my loved ones that help me through the journey, and of course, my Lord and Savior Jesus Christ, whom I thank for everything.

Like the matrix, if you choose to read this book and pick the red peel, your eyes will be open, and you will take a journey into a part of my life. Unlike the matrix, I will not be dodging any bullets, literately. But you will read what it's like through my eyes on how I survive a near-death experience, where I got shot and survive to tell my story; hang on, here we go.

Chapter 1
Family

Hi, my name is Andre Holloway, and I have a remarkable story to tell you. It's about a black teen in the '70s from Compton, California. Now, I'll give you a little background on him; he was a husky young man. In fact, when his mom used to take him to buy clothes, she would have to look in the husky section in the stores. He was the youngest son of three boys and one girl in a family of four children. His sister was the youngest of them all. Although he was husky, his oldest brother was the biggest, so much so, that one of his many nicknames was Heavy. They were all about two years apart. Heavy was about 17 years old on that fateful day. His other brother had a nickname as well: Pookie. Our main character, like his oldest brother, had many nicknames as well, Bustle was one of them. In the neighborhoods where he grew up, and I'm pretty sure in others, there was an older kid that was the leader of the neighborhood kids. He gave him the nickname 'Brussel Butt', he said because of his big butt. When he began to meet other people in the neighborhood and his friends would call out his name, the other people would ask "What did you call him?" And they would say 'Brussel Butt', which was later shortened to just

Brussel. Down the line, those that couldn't say or pronounce Brussel began to say, Bustle.

One of the older girls in the neighborhood couldn't pronounce Brussel or Bustle and began to call him Bubble. Well, Bubble didn't stick that long. It only stuck with her. Bustle became more common for everyone to say so that's how he got his nickname.

Now let's get back to Pookie. Don't think that I was going to let the name Pookie get past you without explaining it. As far as Bustle could remember, Pookie was the only name his brother had at the time. As a matter-of-fact, Bustle didn't even know the meaning of Pookie's name at the time. For all, he knew he got that nickname because he liked to get high on weed, but Bustle did not really know back then that was the meaning of his name. Pookie was 15 years old on that fateful day.

Although Bustle and Pookie were brothers, they were pretty much just the opposite. I'll give you an example: remember I told you that Bustle was a husky young man? Well, Pookie was very slender. Pookie, of course, liked to get high, hang out in the streets, and do a lot of pretty bad things: rob, steal, and gangbang. Bustle, on the other hand, didn't like to do those things. Although he did have one problem, you could say, that was sex. Sex and who he could have sex with were the first things he thought of when he woke up in the morning, and what girl can he get with that day to have sex with. Pookie had a short temper; you could easily get him mad; and he would get out of control. But for Bustle, it would take a whole lot to get him to lose his temper.

One morning in the year 1971, when Bustle was about 7, Pookie was 9, Heavy was 11, and their sister was 5, they were eating breakfast; their mother had made them bacon, sausage, and eggs. And they each had two pieces of bacon and two pieces of sausage. Heavy, being himself, before anyone could start eating, began to drool at the mouth overwhelmingly with desire, would ask if he could have Bustle's bacon and sausage. Although Bustle wanted to keep his bacon and sausage for himself, he knew how much more it meant to his brother Heavy, so he proceeded to give him his bacon and sausage.

Now, Pookie wasn't going for any of that even if he didn't want any extra bacon or sausage; he didn't want Heavy to have it, so they both began to reach for the bacon and sausage. Heavy being the oldest and biggest prevailed. But that didn't stop Pookie; he grabbed the fork off the table and jabbed it into the side of Heavy's stomach. Although it pierced the skin of Heavy's stomach, causing a little blood to appear, it didn't penetrate that deep to cause any serious problems. But it did do one thing for Bustle. It let him know to never get in a fight with his brother Pookie.

The closest they got into a fight was back in the year 1975 when Pookie was 13 and Bustle was 11. They were outside in front of their house on 153rd street in Compton where two of Pookie's gangbanger friends came to pick him up. And in a normal conversation he was having with his brother Pookie, Bustle had said the word blood, and Pookie told Bustle not to say blood around him anymore. Bustle thought he was playing and laughed it off and said blood again, well, he shouldn't have done that. Pookie and his gang buddies began to hit and sock Bustle all over his arms, his legs, his whole body. As he fell to the ground, they began to kick him. Bustle, full of shock and amazement, could not believe that his own brother would harm him in any way just because of the stupid word blood. So other than the normal big brother pushing around and telling little brother what to do, they never fought each other. And I don't call this a fight I'll call this Bustle getting beat down, literally.

Heavy was the pre-Madonna in the family; he would always want the best of everything: shoes, clothes, haircuts. So whatever Heavy got, Pookie made sure he got it too; they got the best of whatever shoe style was popular at the time. Bustle got the cheapest. When his mom would take them to the barbershop, they both got the blowout kit, an afro that made them look like they were a part of The Jackson 5 group. Bustle got the crew cut, the haircut that made him look like he was just about to go to the army. He didn't mind it all that much; he knew his mom had a hard time just paying for Heavy and Pookie to get the things they wanted, and he didn't want to make it any harder for her. He was satisfied with whatever he got.

So now that leaves his sister. His sister didn't have a nickname so we're going to call her Pinkie Tail. She was about 11 years old on that fateful day. Pinkie Tail was a shy and quiet girl with everybody else but Bustle. Even though she was younger than Bustle, she thought she could boss him around, as her two older brothers did. She was the spitting image of their mother, and she wore glasses like her too. It seemed as though she has worn glasses since she started walking. She would suck her two middle fingers most of the time, so much so that Bustle's dad, to prevent her from sucking them, would put hot sauce on her fingers and say, "suck your finger now."

Well, that didn't work because everybody in the house loved the hot sauce on everything, everybody except Bustle. He was the only one that didn't like hot sauce. His dad concocted some type of superhot sauce that he made himself and put on her fingers. No matter what he did, she continued to suck her fingers. Eventually, his dad gave up, and let her do whatever she wanted to do with her fingers.

His dad was a drug dealer; he wasn't like the drug dealers that you see in TV shows, or in the movies with all the glamour. I know his dad was some type of a drug dealer because time and time again, people would come knocking on the door, and his dad would go get his stash and hand them something, and they would give him money. His dad sold weed, pills (I believe they're called amphetamines), and of course, sherm, which is PCP.

His dad didn't only sell drugs; he was a user as well. He remembers so vividly his dad using sherm. One day in the year 1976, when he and his dad were alone at home, he saw his dad smoke some sherm in the kitchen. Then his dad began to act wild. His dad's eyes were lit up and staring into space like he didn't even recognize his son. He began to run into the walls causing dents. He then fell to the floor and began to swing his arms and legs wildly. The drug made him so strong and powerful that he was able to flip the table over while sprawling there on the floor. As Bustle was watching all of this, he felt sad, worried, and most of all, helpless. He ran over to his dad yelling "Daddy, Daddy, are you alright?"

17

All his dad was doing was moaning with a tight jaw and glazed over eyes. He knew his dad couldn't respond to him, but he knew he was in there somewhere.

This wasn't the first time this had happened, but it was the first time the two of them were alone when he got shermed up. Bustle didn't know what to do. The only thing he could remember was that his mom gave his dad milk when he was shermed up before. So, he rushed to the refrigerator in a panic hoping that there was milk in there. To his relief, he found some milk in the refrigerator. He grabbed a glass and poured his dad some milk hoping that it would somehow relax him and bring him out of his wild state.

As his dad was lying on the floor, he put the glass of milk to his lips and tried to force his dad to drink the milk. His dad did not open his mouth, and milk just ran down his face and all over his body. After this failed attempt to calm his dad by giving him milk, his dad started to swing his arms and legs and attempted to get up. After his dad was able to get up, Bustle jumped on his back and held his dad tight from the back to stop him from RAMMING himself into the walls. It was hard because his dad was so strong, but he held onto him and wouldn't let go. It may have been for only 5 minutes, but to a 12-year-old, it seemed to go on for hours. The feeling of helplessness became overwhelming, and Bustle began to cry and asked God to help him keep his daddy from any harm.

Because of this horrifying event, Bustle vowed to never take (or) do any illegal drugs. He had every opportunity to take just about any drug he wanted to since he knew where his dad's stash was. But seeing his dad in that state reminded him never and I mean NEVER EVER use illegal drugs. Matter-of-fact, he hardly ever took any legal drugs, such as aspirin or pain medication, to this day because of what happened.

Bustle loved his mom. One could even call him a mama's boy. He would never want to go and spend the night at a cousin's house or leave his mom. Unfortunately, his mom had mental health problems. She would argue and fuss and cuss out anybody. I mean anybody: Bustle, his brothers and sister, his dad, his aunts, uncles and aunties, neighbors, people on the telephone, County workers, government workers, police officers, everyone, and anyone she would come in contact with. Well, you may think, and some other people may think, this could be a normal reaction. But when you do this out of the blue for no reason at all, something must be wrong. She would always think that everyone was plotting against her or sabotaging everything she tried to do. She would throw pots and pans at Bustle's dad, start fights with him, and beat him up. Bustle knew that his dad could have fought back and hurt his mom, but his dad just sat there and took all that abuse day after day.

Some days, he may have deserved it, but other days he didn't. Bustle's mom went to therapy twice a month and took medication for her illness. As far as he knew, his mom had two major mental breakdowns that she was hospitalized for: one shortly after his little sister was born and another when he was seven or eight years old. During that time, he had to stay with relatives. Those incidents made him protective of her and refused to leave her side. He would always buy her things for her birthday, Mother's Day, and any special occasion that came up, using the little bit of money he earned, just to see a smile on her face. He knew if she wasn't having a nice day that Bustle, or anyone else in the house, wasn't having a nice day either.

Imagine being Bustle at the age of seven in 1971 and you're at home with your mom and siblings. But you don't know where your dad is. And it's at night; you just survived a day of uncertainties; it's bedtime. Although being a kid, you may not like to go to bed, but at least it's one place that you think you're safe from getting in trouble.

As you lay there sleeping, all of a sudden you feel pain. Confused and waking up from a deep sleep you begin to scream and cry because of the pain. You notice an object which looks like a belt rapidly coming toward you. You realize it's your mom, yelling and screaming, and she's actually spanking you, not only you but also your siblings, and screaming, "Wake up, everybody!"

Now Bustle had to go through this several times in his youth. This time was because the living room was a mess, and she made them clean it up, at 1 or 2 o'clock in the morning.

Another time, she woke them up, with another spanking, telling them to look for some item that she was missing. They searched the whole house, for whatever item that was missing, at 2 or 3 o'clock in the morning. A 3rd time, being awakened the same way, at 1 or 2 o'clock in the morning. Someone had broken a drinking glass in the kitchen, and she wanted to know which one of them did it. Well, no one wanted to confess to it. Whether Bustle did it or not, he admitted to it so no one else would get hurt that night.

Speaking of whippings, spankings, or beatings, whatever you want to call them, Pookie received many of them. Bustle's maternal grandmother died in 1951 when his mom was 12 years old, and his grandfather remarried when his mom was still a teenager. They called his grandfather's wife Madea. Bustle's grandparents lived in Texas, and Madea came to California to visit and stayed with Bustle's family in 1971.

Pookie was about 9 years old when she was visiting, and Bustle didn't know the circumstance or what led up to Pookie saying what he said to Madea. But he called Madea a bitch. Madea wasn't timid or one to shy away from any opportunity to administer a good butt whooping to a grandkid that deserved it. But she didn't say a word to Pookie or do anything to him. She told his mother, father, uncle, aunties, and grandfather who was back in Texas what Pookie said to her. One by one, they came over to give him one of those legendary spankings. Except for Bustle's grandfather who was still in Texas. The original plan was that Madea, after visiting, would go back to Texas alone. But Bustle's grandfather arranged and paid the way for his whole family to come back with Madea to Texas, just to give Pookie a spanking in person.

There's no excuse for Pookie to call his grandma a bitch. But there may be a reason, not saying it's okay. In 1967, when Pookie and Bustle were a little bit younger, they were living with their grandparents in Texas. And Bustle was a toddler about 3 years old, so Pookie was about 5. Bustle had just recently been potty-trained and was able to go to the restroom by himself.

One night, Bustle, Pookie, and his grandparents were sitting at the table having dinner. Bustle had to go to the restroom. He didn't quite make it to the toilet in time and because of this one of his turds was left on the restroom floor. When Madea saw the turd, she called Bustle back into the restroom where she made him do something that was unspeakable... EAT. HIS. OWN. TURD! Bustle was only 3 years old, and he didn't know any better, he just did what his grandma told him to do. His brother Pookie witnessed it all, which may be the reason why Pookie called her a bitch, who's to say.

Or who's to say what she may have done to Pookie back then if she was capable of doing that to Bustle. I'll go back even further, who's to say what she may have done to Bustle's mom beginning at the age of 12. The combination of her own mother dying and having a stepmother capable of doing unspeakable things to a 3-year-old, not hard to imagine what Bustle's mom must have gone through that could explain her current mental state.

Chapter 2
His Friends

Bustle had a best friend, and his nickname was Beanie Boy. Beanie Boy was a strong and muscular boy just like Bustle. They were like two peas in the pod. Bustle had more than just one friend in the neighborhood; he had a couple of close friends, two brothers, the younger brother we'll call him Goofy because he looked and acted goofy; he walked funny; and he always did goofy silly things. And the older brother Simon; they called him Simon because of everything that Simon said they did, like the game Simon Says. Simon was the coolest one in the group. He would later reminded me of rapper and actor Will Smith when he first burst onto the scene in the 1980s. Bustle's best friend Beanie Boy was about 12 years old, on that fateful day, Goofy was 13 years old, and Simon was 14 years old. Beanie Boy played a big part in Bustle's life both positively and negatively. Let me tell you how.

Bustle had to hustle for his money, not in a bad way. He didn't get allowances like his friends, Simon, Goofy, or Beanie Boy. One day in 1976, Bustle ordered some greeting cards from his mother's magazines. The deal was that you sell the greeting cards and send most of the money back to the company and keep a small portion for your pay. Well, Bustle didn't plan on sending any money back to the company; he was going to keep all of that money. He got his friends to help him go door-to-door in the neighborhood and sell the greeting cards. He sold them very cheap since he was going to keep all the profit anyway, and he split the money up evenly with his friends.

He also used his dad's lawn mower and went throughout the neighborhood cutting grass. Whenever he met a potential customer with lots of grass that needed to be cut and they turn him down, he made them an offer that they could not refuse, not like a godfather offer, "LOL." He would offer to cut their grass at a very low price so much so that they just could not refuse.

One day after he and his friends were through selling greeting cards, Beanie Boy asked if any of them would like to go to the night service at church with him. Simon said, "no," so Goofy said, "no," then Bustle said, "no."

On another day when Bustle and his friends were finished cutting grass, Beanie Boy asked them again if they would like to come to the night service at church with him. For the second time, Simon said, "no," Goofy said, "no," and Bustle said, "no."

On a different day, they went to the park to play football. When they were finished and on their way home, Beanie Boy asked them once more would they like to come to the night service at church with him. And once again Simon said, "no," and Goofy said, "no," but Bustle decided that he would go this time.

Beanie Boy's parents converted their garage into a church. It had previously been a huge double garage connect. They did a remarkable job in transforming the space into a house of worship. It had a raised altar and pulpit, an area for the piano and the choir to sing, about six rolls of church pews with a walkway in the middle of it, a restroom at the back, and the church was very well lit. And the name of the church was Prayer Time Mission Church of God in Christ. And Beanie Boy's mother was the pastor of the church; she was a real woman of God. God really had his hands on her; she touched so many lives in that neighborhood and in many other neighborhoods as well. Bustle knew that nobody was perfect but with the Lord in your life, leading and guiding your footsteps, that your light would shine. And this woman of God: light was shining bright.

The night that Bustle went to church he felt welcomed, comfortable, and the atmosphere in that place was different, then what was going on outside of the church. There was singing and praying and people testifying about the goodness of God. And Bustle wanted to feel the joy that those Saints were feeling when they prayed, sung, and testified. When the pastor was introduced, she spoke with so much knowledge and authority that you were captivated by every word she said. She preached on John 3:16: "For God so loved the world, that he gave his only begotten Son, that whosoever believed in him should not perish, but have everlasting life."

And on Isaiah 1:18, "Come now, and let us reason together, saith the LORD: though your sins be as scarlet, they shall be as white as snow; though they be red like crimson, they shall be as wool."

She preached that message with so much Power and Anointing from God that the anointing of God was in the church that night.

And Bustle knew that he wasn't living right; he wasn't perfect; and he had a deep dark secret that was haunting him for a long time. He could not believe that anyone could forgive him, or love him, let alone God. But that night, he surrendered and asked God to forgive him. He opened his heart to the Lord, and the Spirit of the Lord touched him. The shame and the pain of that deep dark secret that was haunting him was lifted. He felt the best that he ever felt before; he felt like a new person. Had Beanie Boy not continued to ask him to come to service, he would have missed out on that blessing. Now that's a Positive Act that his best friend Beanie Boy had in his life.

Chapter 3
His Girlfriend

In the year 1977, Bustle had a girlfriend, and her name was Little Piggy. He didn't call her that to be mean; Bustle loved big chubby girls, and she reminded him of the Muppet character Miss Piggy. She would also suck on both of her thumbs, one at a time. While she sucked her thumb, her pointer finger would curl and cover her nose. Little Piggy was about 12 years old, and she was more into sex than Bustle. Before Bustle had moved into the neighborhood, she had been with every other little boy and some girls in the neighborhood already. Bustle was the new kid in town.

Strangely enough, Bustle met Little Piggy in church one Saturday night when they were in choir practice with Beanie Boy, Beanie Boy's two sisters, Money Mae and Moran, and their cousin; we'll call him Blackjack. Money Mae was 11 years; Moran was 14 years; and their cousin Blackjack was 13 years old.

Although Bustle was more physically attracted to Little Piggy, there was something about Money Mae. When he looked into her eyes, it lured him close to her; he felt a deeper attraction to her more than just physical. When Little Piggy noticed that Bustle was interested in Money Mae,

Little Piggy decided to convince Money Mae to write a note with her to give to Bustle. The note said which one of them Little Piggy or Money Mae, did he like and would like to be his girlfriend. He decided on Money Mae for previous reasons.

Little Piggy wasn't going to give up that easily; she was relentless. She asked Bustle to meet her in the church restroom. For some strange reason, he agreed. Bustle went to the restroom first, and shortly after, Little Piggy followed. When she entered the restroom where Bustle was waiting, she attempted to persuade him to change his mind, by kissing him and allowing him to caress her body. Although Bustle did those things, he had made his decision and was going to stick to it.

Now, I did mention that Little Piggy was relentless; she had another plan. She convinced Money Mae's cousin, Blackjack, to persuade Bustle to change his mind and pick her, Little Piggy, instead of Money Mae. She promised Blackjack that if he could convince Bustle, she would set him up with her friend. We'll call her Buttback because her butt seemed like it was on her back; she was 12 years old.

Blackjack began to convince Bustle to choose Little Piggy instead of his cousin Money Mae, by telling him that he would never be able to date his cousin because of his aunt and uncle. They would not allow her to date at her age. And then he said that Bustle wouldn't even have an opportunity to have sex with Money Mae. On the other hand, with Little Piggy, he could do any and all things he desired to do with her. Now that's all he needed to hear.

Little Piggy was not just relentless but also conniving; she had no intentions of hooking up her friend Buttback

28

with Blackjack. After Blackjack convinced Bustle to pick Little Piggy, Little Piggy asked Bustle to hook his friend Goofy up with Buttback.

One evening, in that same year 1977, when the sun was going down, and the moonlight shining and you could see the stars sparkling in the distance and you could hear the pretty sounds of birds chirping and a pleasant calmness filled the night air. Skirrrrrrrrrrrrt! Not so, we're talking about Compton California, in the '70s. It was one evening when the sun was going down, but you could barely see the moonlight, and you couldn't see any stars because of the smog. Instead of the sounds of birds chirping, there were the sounds of helicopters and police sirens, ambulance racing down the street, gunfire, and maybe a couple of people screaming in the distance. But that was a typical evening. Bustle and his friends were accustomed to hearing sounds like that.

Bustle, Little Piggy, Goofy, and Buttback met at a vacant house in the neighborhood.

Bustle and Little Piggy were in one room; Goofy and Buttback were in another room. Bustle and Little Piggy proceeded to have sex. And after 10 minutes or more, Little Piggy made a suggestion. She said that they should switch partners. Bustle wasn't having any of that, but I did say that Little Piggy was relentless, conniving, and now she was a freak and super nasty. She pressed on and on about it so that Bustle just gave in, unwillingly though. So Little Piggy went into the other room where Goofy and Buttback were and proceeded to tell them that they were switching partners.

Buttback came into the room where Bustle was. Now, it wasn't that Bustle wasn't attracted to Buttback; it's just that he didn't believe in switching partners at that time. He looked at Buttback and told her that he was not going to have sex with her. She agreed so they waited and talked there for five minutes or less. And in the distance, they could hear the faint sounds of love-making going on in the other room. A few seconds later, Little Piggy, while sucking her thumb and her finger curled over her nose, walked into the room where Bustle and Buttback were, Goofy following behind her, walking funny using a T-shirt to cover his obvious boner that was still erect and poking through his shirt. Bustle seeing this immediately ran out of the vacant house and ran home.

Another day, when all four of them decided to play hooky: Bustle, Little Piggy, Goofy, and Buttback. They agreed to meet at Buttback's house because Buttback parents both worked in the daytime, so no one would be home during school hours. We know that Little Piggy was relentless, conniving, and super freaky, but now she was also creative. Of course they played house but with a little twist. The husbands (Bustle and Goofy) were not allowed to have sex with the wives (Buttback and Little Piggy). The only way that Bustle or Goofy could have sex with them is if they left the room as husbands and came back as strangers to rape them.

Buttback must have mentioned to Little Piggy that Bustle did not have sex with her back at the vacant house. Because Little Piggy insisted that they switch partners again. Bustle was not interested in that. But Little Piggy was persistent, so they made an agreement that they would switch partners but only take five humps and then switch back.

They had so much fun that day; they decided to do it again the next day. This time, before Bustle and Goofy got to Buttback's house, Little Piggy and Buttback met them on the way and told them that they were not sure if the house was empty. Bustle and Goofy approached the front door of Buttback's house as if to knock on the door and ask if Buttback was home. When they got to the front door and knocked, the door just crept open. Bustle and Goofy got scared and ran away. Shortly afterward, they saw Buttback's dad come out of the house and drive down the street.

Chapter 4
That Fateful Day

Bustle didn't remember exactly what day it was in 1977, but it was a school day because he didn't go to school that day. He was supposed to, but he played hooky. Matter-of-fact, I don't think his parents were home the night before or that day. The reason why he didn't think his parents were home the night before or that day is because the night before, Bustle and his girlfriend Little Piggy had sex in his parent's bedroom and in their bed. He remembers so well because it was the first time he had sex with all his clothes off.

Previously, it was humping girls with his clothes on or just pulling them down to his knees. So back to that day, sometime that afternoon, Bustle went over to Beanie Boy's house. When he got there, Beanie Boy and his little sister Money Mae was the only ones home. They were in the living room talking for 5 minutes or less. Money Mae was sitting on the couch, and Beanie Boy was standing by his parent's bedroom doorway, 2 or 3 feet away, and Bustle about 5 steps away from them. Beanie Boy walked into his parent's bedroom and came out with a 12-gauge shotgun, unloaded it, and showed it to Bustle. Although Bustle was curious, he was scared to be there. Then his friend reloaded the shotgun and pointed the gun at his sister's face. She screamed out with a loud voice, "Stop."

Then he pointed the gun at Bustle, and Bustle said, "Stop playing man. I'm leaving."

And just as he was walking toward the kitchen, which was 2 steps away from him, also the way out to the back door, Beanie Boy said, "Wait, I'm coming with you." And then it happened. Bustle did not hear the gun go off. It was like it was in slow motion; he felt the force slowly carry him into the kitchen, as he flipped over and landed head first on the floor with the back of his head. His feet propped up on the oven; he began to hear squirting sounds, as blood was gushing out of his chest. He could hear the muffled sound of Money Mae screaming and Beanie Boy hovering over him, asking him if he was okay? And all he could think of is that he was very tired, so he said, "I'm okay I just need some rest."

The gunshot had blown a hole in his chest. The 12-gauge shotgun shell had one big metal pellet and a lot of little metal pellets. The big pellet went all the way through his chest and came out the back, cracking his left shoulder blade, extracting his left pectoral muscle, and missing his heart by 2 inches as the little pellets exploded inside also missing his heart.

His eyes were dilated, but he was still conscious and as he laid there and realized that he just got shot! He began to think of all the sins that he committed. And that he was not worthy of God's love and if he were to die that day that he would surely be lost.

As Beanie Boy began to search for someone to help them, he ran outside and saw Bustle's brother, Pookie, and yelled to him, "I just shot your brother!"

Pookie did not believe him and continue walking down the street.

Money Mae called her parents at work who owned a thrift store, not far from their house. Her dad answered the phone, Mr. Deacon T; he was the deacon of Prayer Time Mission Church. And she began to explain what happened. When he got off the phone with his daughter, he immediately called 911 and rushed home. His wife, the woman of God and Pastor of Prayer Time Mission Church, gathered the few Saints that were visiting her at the thrift store and began to unleash the Power of Faith through prayer right there at the thrift store.

Bustle continued to think about his situation; while Bible scriptures were going through his mind, he thought to himself, "If I repent and ask God to forgive me of all my sins, I won't be lost."

So, he repented in his heart and asked God to forgive him of all of his sins. His eyes still dilated and conscious, still lying there, waiting to die but at peace with himself because he just repented. He began to think some more about his life. His dream ever since he was a little boy, believe it or not, was to be married, have a wife and children, at least a little boy.

As he lay there, he knew he'd never have a chance to experience that if he were to die that day. Then out of nowhere, it seemed, he thought to himself, "If God has the Power, the Might, and Ability to forgive me of all of my sins, then surely, he has the Power, the Might, and Ability to allow me another chance at life."

He asked God to spare his life and give him another chance, a chance to get married, have a wife, and have a son. And to be alive a couple of more years just to be with them.

Meanwhile, Beanie Boy's father, Deacon T, had arrived just before the paramedics arrived. Now, Bustle could not see, but he could sense and hear what was going on. The paramedics entered the kitchen where Bustle was lying. They took one look at him, grab one side, lifted him, and said, "It went all the way through" and dropped his body like a sack of potatoes and said, "He's a goner; he's not going make it."

Their plans were just to leave him lying there for the coroner, but Deacon T pleaded with the paramedics to take him to the hospital anyway. Reluctantly, they complied with his wishes.

As the paramedics were carrying Bustle out of the house, he could hear his brother Pookie and his sister yelling and screaming at Beanie Boy and Money Mae saying, "If my brother dies, you will die!"

Now they were headed to Martin Luther King Junior Hospital, which was known as "Killer King." There were a lot of stories about Killer King. One of the stories that Bustle remembers, whether it's true or not, is that a man went to Killer King with only a broken arm, and in their care, the man died. Of course, there were many other stories that were told, which enabled them to get their reputation. But it didn't matter that Bustle was going to Killer King because prayer went out already on his behalf.

Not only did the woman of God, the Pastor of Prayer Time Mission Church and their members pray for Bustle. But word spread, through the neighborhood, that Bustle had gotten shot and was clinging on to life, that they all prayed for him. Even his dad prayed to God. It was told to Bustle later. That his dad went out in the backyard and got down on his knees, looked up to heaven, and asked God to spare his son Bustle's life. Proclaiming he would gladly trade his own life in exchange for Bustle's life saying, "Take me not him." It didn't matter what hospital Bustle was going to, the Power of Prayer was with him.

As the paramedics pulled into the emergency area of the hospital in a hectic panic rushing Bustle through the emergency doors. Still conscious and eyes still dilated, he could hear gut-curdling screams, as he was being rolled into the operating room. As the doctor began to direct nurses and orderlies into position, he could hear the sound of glass breaking, and the doctor saying, "There's no time for that, anyway he's in shock; he won't feel anything." To Bustle's amazement, he assumed that what had broken was the anesthetic medication.

Bustle could feel the medical staff grabbing his legs and arms and cutting away his clothing, as they administered the endotracheal intubation tube down his throat. He could also hear a lot of gasping sounds, of amazement coming from either the staff maybe even the doctor himself as they hastily performed the operation. Bustle could feel them position his body onto the opposite side of the gunshot wound. They grabbed his left arm and pulled it over his head. Made an incision, from the middle of his chest around the side to the middle of his back. Then up the middle of his back, until it reached his shoulder blade.

This was just the beginning of the immense pain that he had to endure. As he laid there trying to scream yet unable to because of the tube down his throat, he felt his arm seem like it came farther away from his body. As he lay there, doubt began to creep through his mind. Maybe God did not hear his prayer? He thought. Then the most excruciating pain he ever felt before hit him hard. The doctor had to cut his rib out in order to get to his lung to repair it.

Unable to scream, he grunted within himself he wished with all his might that he was anywhere else but there. Then that excruciating pain hit him again, now it's getting serious. The current pain made getting shot feel like a tickle. It was unbearable. Bustle was still conscious maybe the doctors did not know that, and there was no way for Bustle to let them know either; he had a tube down his throat; he had lost a lot of blood; and he felt overwhelmed with hopelessness. He thought to himself, "If I'm going to die, please let me die right now!" And that was the last thing that he remembered, that day.

Chapter 5
Recovery at the Hospital

This young man lay in the hospital bed with two IVs, one in each arm, a catheter, a tube down his throat, and two tubes on the left side of his torso to drain fluid from his body. Bustle slowly regained consciousness and found himself waking up in a hospital bed. Faintly seeing his mom, a couple of relatives, and close friends hovering over his hospital bed. He was unable to speak to them because of the tube down his throat. He just gestured to them by moving his head and smiling. That's all he remembers from that day.

The next day, he needed another surgery. This time, it wasn't a near-death situation, and they were able to put him to sleep. He needed a tube inserted all the way through his chest, where the shotgun wound was. This tube was between 8 and 10 inches long and had tiny holes all around the middle of it. And it was thick as a water hose. After the surgery, the nurses had to clean and sterilize his wound using a cleaning solution of hydrogen peroxide inserting it into the tube with a big plastic syringe, and they had to do this daily.

One day while he was still in the hospital, some detectives came by to ask him some questions. They wanted to know if it was an accident like Beanie Boy and Money Mae said it was. Unable to speak, he nodded his head as if to say yes it was an accident.

They wrote a few things down on their notepad and departed. The first tube the doctors took out of Bustle was the endotracheal intubation tube that was down his throat. It left his throat raw and irritated; he had some form of laryngitis; he could barely speak. One of his nurses would force him to speak louder or she would not help him. She requested that he call her 'mama' to get her attention. He thought at first that she was just being mean to him, but he soon realized that she was making him do that for his own benefit. Although it was painful, he slowly regained his speech. Bustle's mom would visit him quite often, if not every day.

One day, the woman of God, the pastor of Prayer Time Mission Church and two of her daughters, Money Mae and Moran, came to visit Bustle. Although getting shot was a negative event for Bustle, that Beanie Boy played a major part in; he was still concerned about his best friend's state of mind. The family had told Bustle that Beanie Boy was not eating and was depressed since he got shot. Bustle pleaded with Beanie's mom to tell him to come to visit him. He wanted to let Beanie Boy know that he had no ill will toward him; everything was okay and that he didn't want to lose his friendship because of what happened.

The next time Beanie Boy's parents visited Bustle, he was with them and a big smile came on Bustle's face as he greeted his best friend. Beanie Boy immediately came out of that depression when he saw the big smile on Bustle's face. They embraced, as Beanie Boy repeatedly apologize for what he had done. Bustle assured him that everything was good between them.

Bustle had now been in the hospital for about a week and a half. He woke up one morning and looked at his hands; his hands didn't look like they were his hands anymore. He had nice plump thick hands before; these were flat and skinny hands that he saw. For some reason, sadness begins to feel his heart; he didn't like to see his hands look that way. Bustle began to cry as he was looking at his hands and saying, "What's happening to me?" Bustle was losing weight; he had never been that thin before.

Since the time that Bustle was in the hospital, he had to regain his vision, learn how to speak again, and now that the doctors were removing the catheter, he had to learn how to walk again, to get to the restroom. He began to have a daily routine: wake up, eat, and drink his breakfast, which so happen to taste like baby food, get his bandages changed and his gunshot wound clean and sterilized, go to physical therapy to learn to walk again, and most of all the dreaded breathing therapy for his lungs, the one that you would have to inhale into a plastic casing with a ball in it to make it levitate to a certain point, which it was one of the most painful and hardest ordeals of the recovery. This went on for several weeks.

And for Bustle's recreation time, his mother would bring him playing cards, puzzles, and some model cars with the glue kit so he could put them together. The next tubes that were removed from Bustle were the two that were on his side that drained fluid. The doctors put him to sleep to do that operation.

Bustle grew tired and weary of being in the hospital and long for the opportunity to go home so every time the doctors came by to check on him, he would ask them, "When can I go home?"

And time and time again, they would say, "When your lungs get stronger." Bustle would work harder and harder on his breathing therapy. But he couldn't go home as long as he had that tube through his wound in his chest.

One day when his doctor was visiting him and checking on the tube through his chest, the doctor began to examine it and wiggled it around a little. Bustle would jump and flinch every time the doctor touched it because of the pain. The doctor began to strike up a conversation with Bustle to distract him.

While Bustle was talking and in mid-sentence, the doctor yanked the tube from his chest, and Bustle felt like he had pulled his soul right out of his chest. He did it so quickly that Bustle didn't have time to realize what was happening. And it was so painful that he felt like he just got shot, all over again. The doctor prescribed pain medication to help when needed, and after six weeks in the hospital, Bustle could finally go home. The nurses had to show his mom the proper way to clean, sterilize, and change his bandages, and after his mom learned to care for and clean his wound, he went home.

Chapter 6
Recovery at Home

Bustle was home, and his mom took good care of him. She waited on him hand and foot. She got him whatever he wanted. She was happy; he was home, still alive, and had survived that dreadful day. She kept him supplied with Nabisco Ginger Snaps and Welch's grape juice. His favorite foods, such as grilled ham and cheese sandwich with a sliced pickle on the side and his favorite ice cream, Butter Pecan.

Although he was getting all of those goodies and treats, he was still in severe pain most of the time. His mom would give him the pain medication when he was in pain, but he realized that when he took the medication, the pain would subside, but it would come back quicker and more fierce. But if he neglected to take the medication, he noticed that the pain would subside slowly, and the pain would come back less severe. So, he eventually endured the pain for a while so he didn't have to depend on taking the pain medication.

They even brought him a small color TV to put in his room. Unlike the last time, they brought him a TV; he got to keep this one. Two years before, on Bustle's birthday in the summer of 1975, when he turned 11, his dad told his mom that he was taking Bustle to buy him a birthday present. They got in the car and drove to the department store where Bustled picked out the TV that he wanted and his dad went up to the counter to pay for it, pulled out his checkbook, and wrote a check for the purchase of the TV. They got back in the car and drove off. Bustle's dad pulled into a pawnshop parking lot, grabbed Bustle's brand-new TV, and pawned it for cash. Bustle was confused he thought his dad bought the TV for his birthday present. I mean that's what he told him.

Well, his dad was about to tell him something else. His dad told him that they were going to the horse race track for his birthday, and he told his son to pick a horse, and he would bet two dollars on it for him. Well, his dad bet $2 for him and made his own bets as well.

Surprise! Bustle's horse won, but his dad's horse didn't. Did Bustle get the money for his horse winning? No.

That's why Bustle was happy he got his own TV when he got home from the hospital. Yes, it was finally his time to get what he wanted from his mom and dad because his brother Heavy had moved out already and was living with their Aunt Annie. He had the bedroom to himself practically because his brother Pookie was hardly at home anyway, due to running the streets all day and all night.

One night, everyone was home sleeping, except Pookie. It was after midnight when Pookie barreled through the front door rushing to the bedroom where Bustle was sleeping. Immediately taking off his shirt, pants, and shoes leaving only his underwear on and jumped into his own bed. After a few seconds, you could hear police sirens and the

43

sound of someone knocking very loudly on the front door. Bustle's mom and dad got up to answer the door, and it was several police officers standing at the front door.

One of the officers demanded to see all the young men in the house. Then several officers rushed into the bedroom where Bustle and Pookie were sleeping and pulled them both out of the bed, Bustle could hardly see what was going on because of the bright flashlights shining in his eyes. The officers took Pookie away that night; they would have taken Bustle also. But in his condition, there was no way he had been outside the house that night or any other recent night.

One day, when Bustle's mom and dad had an appointment to go to, they had to leave Bustle at home. His mom asked Little Piggy if she could come over and take care of Bustle while they were gone. Little Piggy came over and went into the bedroom where Bustle was and sat on his bed next to him. Bustle was glad to see his girlfriend but he was very nervous.

God had spared his life, and he wanted to do the right thing. But when Little Piggy began to kiss his lips, he thought to himself, "Well, maybe I might be too young to live a saved life," and they began to have sex.

When Bustle's parents got home, his mom went into his bedroom, saw Little Piggy in the bed with him, smiled, and just walked out of the room.

Weeks went by. Bustle's mom had been changing his bandages and cleaning his gunshot wound daily. And he had been going to his doctor's appointment once a week. When he was at the hospital for a doctor's appointment, the doctor had told Bustle's mom that the gunshot wound was taking too long to heal and suggested that they allow him to do a skin graft operation. Bustle was a little hesitant about it at first. Because the doctor said that he was not going to put him to sleep but that he would numb the area where he was going to perform the operation. The doctor had said that he would like to do the operation while his patient was conscious as could be helped to reduce the possibility of unseen complications. Bustle got the operation and stayed in the hospital for about two days.

After the skin graft operation and his stay in the hospital, Bustle did not have to wear bandages over his wound anymore; the skin from his thigh cover the exposed flesh on his chest.

Two or three days after Bustle came home from the hospital, the skin on his chest began to shrink, tighten up, and got darker, like it was dying. And when he went back to the doctor, he said to Bustle, "The skin graft may or may not adapt, but if you want, I could do another skin graft or take your chances and use cocoa butter to rub over your skin daily, that may help." Bustle took his chances on using cocoa butter daily.

Before Bustle got shot, he played pee-wee football at Enterprise Park so Bustle was anxious to get back to playing football again. But he was concerned because he was not able to stand up straight yet. Although he was walking and moving slow, he was slumped over to the left side at almost a 45° angle, his hand and arm almost touch the ground like he had a weight on that side forcing him in that position.

The next time Bustle had a doctor's appointment, he asked his doctor, "When can I play football again."

And his doctor explained to him that he had no pictorial muscle on the left side of his chest and that he was missing two ribs that were protecting the left side of his chest also his shoulder blade was cracked in half. And that if he were to get hit on that side it could be harmful to him and that he might not survive. The doctor suggested that he forget about ever playing football again. Bustle was sad to hear that news.

Bustle's mom suggested that the doctor put him on some type of disability; she feared that he may never be able to work ever. But the doctor said no to that. He didn't want to handicap Bustle and cause him to rely on disability. He told Bustle that he was still young; he had his whole future ahead of him. But he also told Bustle that he had to work very hard at his physical therapy, if he did not try to lift his arm over his head to stretch his body, that he may stay in that position for the rest of his life.

Chapter 7
The Breakup

Bustle had an old raggedy shack in his backyard, made of wood, where his dad used to keep a lot of old tools and junk. Since he thought his parents were pretty much allowing him to do anything, he decided to clean and fix up that old raggedy shack and use it for his love shack. He had some old bunk beds that his parents were going to throw away, but Bustle decided to use them instead. He divided the bunk beds to make twin beds and use them for his shack. He found some unused carpet and put it on the floor of the shack and got some old sheets that his mother wasn't using anymore and put them over the windows, he even got an old lamp that didn't have a shade cover over it and use that as well.

Bustle called Little Piggy over to his backyard to take a look at what he did to his shack, for them to have some fun in and some privacy.

Little Piggy began to come over so often that she became friends with Bustle's little sister. Well, Little Piggy asked Bustle to hook his sister up with one of his friends. Well, we know how persuasive Little Piggy can be, so Bustle got his best friend Beanie Boy to come and be with his sister. The two couples (Bustle, Little Piggy, his sister, and Beanie Boy) were in the shack having sex. After 10 minutes or so, Little Piggy asked Bustle to go get her a glass of water out of the house. When Bustle returned with the glass of water, Little Piggy and Beanie Boy were in the bed together having sex. Well, this infuriated Bustle; he didn't want to have anything to do with his friend, Beanie Boy, or his girlfriend, Little Piggy.

A day or two later Little Piggy came back over to Bustle's house to make up with him. She had bought him bags of goodies, popcorn, candy, soda pop, cupcakes, cheese puffs all of his favorite things. He wondered how did she get all of that stuff. He knew she like to shoplift, but it didn't look like she could've shoplifted all of these items. Well, he soon found out how she did it. Little Piggy and her friends had made photocopies of dollar bills, and they had taken them up to the laundry mat and put them in the coin change machine and got quarters; yes, this was way back when technology wasn't as good as it is today.

Bustle got back with Little Piggy, and they were back at it again. This time, Bustle had to get Goofy to be with his sister.

Bustle's posture began to get a little bit better, although he still couldn't raise his arm over his head and he still was leaning to the side, he was improving.

One day, he saw his girlfriend Little Piggy with one of Beanie Boy's older brothers, walking down the street, up toward the intersection. He decided to follow them.

Unaware that Bustle was following them, they proceeded to enter a motel parking lot. He watched as they entered one of the motel rooms. Bustle saddened and feeling a little bit jealous ran home and couldn't wait to see what she had to say about that.

He saw her the next day and questioned her about it. They began to argue, and when the argument got more heated up, she began to throw blows. Bustle not wanting to hurt her, or maybe get hurt himself, held her tight to stop her from hitting him. Only able to use the one side of his body, she bit him so he let her go. That was one of many altercations that they went through in their relationship. They got back together.

Bustle began to think about his relationship with Little Piggy. He thought if he stayed with Little Piggy that he would be the so-called typical black man that allowed his woman to get on the county, have a bunch of kids, and wait every month for a check to come in, to take care of them. He decided that he didn't want to be that type of black man.

Chapter 8
Alison

Bustle started to hang out more with his friend Alison; he was the same age as Bustle. Alison became Bustle's new best friend. Alison was light-skinned; he looked like he could be the son of Lionel Richie from the Commodores. He had a Schwinn bike that he fixed up to become the best bike in the neighborhood. Alison had like a low rider bike it had a lot of truck lights on it, a lot of chrome parts, he even made a box to hold the speakers for his 8-track tape player. He painted his bike candy apple red; it was beautiful. He cherished his bike; it was the envy of all the neighborhood.

One day, a reporter from the city of Compton came down to take pictures of Alison's bike and him. He wrote an article and put it in the town paper; it was one of the proudest highlights that happened in the neighborhood. Alison began to help Bustle fix his bike up; Bustle had a Huffy mini 10-speed bike; they would go to the neighborhood auto parts shop and buy truck lights for their bikes. Bustle's bike wasn't nearly as elaborated as Alison's bike, but Alison was going to help him get it as close as he could to it.

Alison had shown Bustle where to buy a donut steering wheel for their bikes. Alison had extended handlebars, but he was also going to put a donut steering wheel on it as well. They also build model cars together. Alison showed Bustle how to convert the model car that his mom brought him when he was in the hospital into a low rider using a miniature motor hooked up to a 9-volt battery with a string attached to the wheels and the frame of the model car. They were always together every day for months either working on their bikes, model cars, or just hanging out trying to get with girls; they were inseparable.

Then one day, Bustle stayed home from school; he was sick. Alison had come over to visit; he didn't go to school either that day. They hung out and talked for about 30 minutes; then Alison said to Bustle, "Come over to my house for a little while, I have something I want to show you."

Bustle told him, "I'm still kind of feeling pretty bad; maybe I'll come over later on today."

Then Alison told him, "Well, I guess no girls for you today man," and smiled and giggled as he normally does. Then left and went home.

Later that day before school was out, Bustle decided to go over to Alison's house who lived on the same street as Bustle. Bustle stayed on 153rd street near Nester. Alison lived on 153rd near Central Avenue. Bustle got to Alison's house and knocked on the door, but no one would answer, although he heard somebody in the house. He called out for Alison, but no answer. He looked in the window by the front door but couldn't see anything. He went around to the side of the house and looked into another window, which viewed the dining room area. He could barely see inside the house, but he thought he seen somebody tied up to the dining room table legs. But he wasn't sure; then he went back home.

It was sometime after school around about 3:30 PM that Bustle saw police cars, fire trucks, and paramedics down the street where Alison lived. He ran down the street to see what was going on, as other people were coming to see as well. When he got to Alison's house, there was a crowd of people around his house, and some people were saying that they found a body in the house, and it was Alison. Bustle could not believe it; he just talked to Alison a few hours ago. His friend could not be dead. And the crowd began to discuss what could have happened.

Someone said, "They could not find Alison's bike and that whoever killed him must have tied him up, sliced his face, cut his stomach open, slit his throat, and stole his bike."

This made Bustle so very sad. He wondered if he went home with Alison, maybe he would still be alive or maybe both of them would be dead.

Chapter 9
Fighting

The year was 1978, and Bustle attended Enterprise Junior High School, in Compton, California. It was the first day of school, and Bustle was a little concerned because on the last day of school the semester before, he was playing cards with Ricky May and some other classmates. They were playing for money IOUs. Bustle was losing big-time, but he realized they were cheating him.

One of Ricky May's friends was sitting behind Bustle and telling Ricky everything that Bustle had in his hands. Bustle didn't realize it until it was too late. When the bell ring for them to go home, Ricky said to Bustle, "I want my money next time I see you."

Bustle had no plans of paying Ricky May anything. He knew when he saw Ricky May again that they were going to fight because Bustle wasn't going to back down from any fight; his father made sure of that.

Sometime in September 1973, when Bustle was about nine years old and his sister seven, they attended Martin Luther King Jr. elementary school, in Watts. There was a student named Boulder. Bustle didn't know if that was his real name, but he was and look just like a rock. He had cuts under his eyes like a boxer. His knuckles were all callous because he had been in many fights, and he was as solid as a rock. He was a much older kid than Bustle because he was sent back two grade levels. He was the definition of the word bully He terrorized every kid he came in contact with.

One day, he confronted Bustle and told him, "Give me all your money."

Bustle didn't have any money to give him so he said, "Next time I see you, you better have some money for me, or I'm going to kick your ass."

Bustle had a hard time trying to get any money for himself. He definitely wasn't going to be trying to get any money to give it to somebody else, so he had to avoid Boulder. Every day after school, he would rush out of his classroom, run to his sister's classroom, grab her, and run home evading and avoiding Boulder. One day, Boulder was hot on their trail. Bustle and his sister hid on the side of an abandoned house. Bustle was breathing and panting very fast, and his sister was confused and wondering what was going on, as he was praying for Boulder not to find them. When they got home, his parents wondered why they were late getting home, and his sister told them what had happened.

Bustle's dad was infuriated and said, "No son of mine is going to be running away from a fight."

He beat Bustle with a belt as he was yelling at him, "If you ever ran away from a fight again, I'm going to beat you even harder next time!"

When Bustle got to school the next day, he told all his friends that he was not going to run away from Boulder again. The word got out; Boulder found out and confronted

Bustle, in front of the school, after school, and said, "So I hear you're not going to run away from me anymore," and poked Bustle in his chest with his finger and pushed him away. Bustle push Boulder back and Boulder looked at Bustle with a smirk and grin and sock Bustle right in the jaw.

Well, just like in the cartoons, Bustle heard bells ringing, birds chirping, and it seemed like the earth was moving under his feet. But that didn't stop Bustle; Boulder had turned around and was walking away; then Bustle ran and jumped on his back and started socking him in the head. Boulder threw Bustle off his back and proceeded to get on top of him and throw several punches at him, and finally, an adult came and separated the two of them. Bustle wasn't going to run away from any fights ever again. Even though Bustle still was recovering from the gunshot accident, he wasn't going to let Ricky May know about it.

Bustle knew that you are not supposed to let your enemy know that you are vulnerable. He learned that several months earlier when he met Calvin Small at school. He had a sister named Sheila Small that Bustle was very attracted to, so he befriended Calvin to get close to Sheila. Although their last name was small, there was nothing about them that was small. Calvin was yoked and muscular like Bustle used to be, and Sheila was voluptuous in all the right places. She had a nice apple bottom butt and double D breast. While Bustle was hanging out with Calvin at school, Sheila came over to talk with Calvin. Then Bustle decided to make his move; he started flirting with her telling her how wonderful she was and how beautiful she looked. He asked if he could walk her home from school; she agreed. They talked about a lot of things along the way, and when they got to her house, she invited him in.

Her mom was still at work so they were in the house alone. Bustle wasted no time and asked her the big question he said, "Would you like to be my lady?"

She said happily, "Yes, I would."

He smiled and said, "Well, to make it official, we need to kiss."

She said, "I don't like kissing," and that smile that he had turned into a frown.

Bustle said, "Well, what can we do to seal the deal?"

She grabbed him by the hand and lead him into her mother's bedroom. Then unbuckled his pants, pulled them down to his ankles, took her pants off, her panties off, and laid on the bed. Then pulled Bustle down to her outspread legs. As he began to penetrate her, he thought to himself, "This is a pleasant surprise, I'm getting more than I asked for."

But that was short-lived, they could hear the front door opening and the sound of Sheila's mom entering the house, calling out, "Sheila come here."

She threw Bustle off her, with his pants still down to his ankles. Grabbed him and put him in the hallway closet, while she ran to go see what her mother wanted, telling him to be quiet and not to say a word.

He was terrified, too scared to even pull his pants up, pondering what to do. He had to make a decision right away, as soon as he heard her mother walk past the hallway closet and into her room. He said to himself, "Now, this is my chance."

He opened the closet door while his pants were still down to his ankles, grabbing them while stumbling toward the front door, not yet having his pants fully on, ran through the front yard as he was buckling his pants up, Sheila's little neighbor kids shouted out, "He was f**king Sheila!" And laughing while Bustle ran home as fast as he could.

The next day was a Saturday, Bustle rode his bike over to Calvin and Sheila's house. Really wanting to hang out with Sheila but unable to, went bike riding to the park with Calvin instead. Bustle riding his bike far ahead of Calvin approach one of his archenemies, a boy that he used to prevent from bullying smaller kids, with two of his henchmen.

Bustle stopped his bike in front of all three of them, nervous about what could happen to him, began to reason with them by saying, "Hey man, I'm in no condition to be fighting now. I'm recovering from getting shot a couple of months ago."

His archenemy's eyes lit up with no compassion for Bustle's circumstance, raised the baseball bat that he had with him, reared back, and was ready to swing it. When Calvin came up behind Bustle on his bike and said, "What's going on here?"

Since Calvin arrived with his muscular bodybuilding figure, Bustle's arch-enemy the coward that he is lowered the baseball bat and said, "Nothing man," and took his two henchmen and walked away.

Bustle knew from that point never to expect any sympathy from anybody, especially your enemies.

So, when Bustle came across Ricky May that first day of school, before the bell ring for class to start, Bustle was ready. He wasn't going to back down and not going to expect any sympathy from Rickey May and told him, "I don't owe you anything."

Ricky May threw a punch and caught Bustle's jaw slightly. Then Bustle threw a punch back and connected to the side of Ricky May's left eye socket, and the teachers and counselors separated the two young men, and Ricky May had a bruise on the side of his eye socket till this day. Every time they saw each other, they would fight; passing down the hall going to class, in the lunchroom, even when Bustle showed up for school football tryouts, he and Ricky May would fight. The coach had to let one of them go; unfortunately, it was Bustle.

Chapter 10
The Party

It was late 1978, Buttback was becoming 14 years of age, and her parents allowed her to have a birthday party that night. And all her friends were invited: Bustle, Goofy, Simon, Blackjack, Little Piggy, Sykes, Beanie Boy and even his two sisters Money Mae and Moran who were able to come to the party, her next-door neighbors Sheila Reddy and Lisa Reddy, and a lot more people in the neighborhood and her family and friends.

Buttback's parents had a big covered patio in their backyard where they set up most of the food. They also had a live DJ that was playing the song *Slide* by the group Slave when Bustle notice that Money Mae was there at the party, looking gorgeous. He couldn't remember what type of blouse she had on, but he could definitely remember she had the tightest pair of white slacks on that he had ever seen before. When the DJ began playing slow jams, Bustle grabbed Money Mae, went on the dance floor, and before the night was over his handprints were all over that white pair of slacks literally. That was a great party; everyone had a remarkable time. No one was fighting, no arguments, no one complained about that party at all. It went so well that the next month Sheila Reddy and Lisa Reddy decided to have a party too.

All the same characters were there, besides Beanie Boy and his two sisters Money Mae and Moran. Bustle was wearing his favorite outfit, rust-colored slacks with a silk shirt, that was rust-colored and white with a pattern design. It had been a year and one day exactly from the day he first got shot. Bustle was feeling good about this party. He met up with Simon, Goofy, Sykes, and AT. AT was Bustle's next-door neighbor. He was the first friend he had when Bustle and his family moved into the neighborhood. AT was a year older than Bustle, the same age as Simon and Sykes.

Now, Sheila and Lisa before they had their party were proclaiming that their party was going to be better than Buttback's party, and again Buttback's party was awesome, so they had big shoes to feel sadly they came up way too short. Buttback's party was outside in the backyard where there was plenty of room to dance and mingle. Sheila and Lisa's party was in their house, in the living room; it was small and crowded. But that didn't stop Bustle; he was ready to dance. All of his friends were just hanging out on the wall, so he was the first one to ask somebody to dance. While he was dancing, he noticed a commotion going on; some guys from another neighborhood came to crash the party. Simon and some more neighborhood guys threw them out of the party, and they all went running down the street.

The party began to migrate outside in the front yard and also in the street in front of Lisa and Sheila's house. They live three houses down from the corner of 152nd, street and Nestor. It was a calm and cool pleasant night. There was laughter in the wind as the partygoers began to discuss the incident that just recently happened. Bustle was in the street performing a dance called 'poplocking.'

Then it happened out of nowhere shotgun fire rang out. Bustle hit the ground, he did not just fall on the ground on purpose; a force took him to the ground. The crowd began to scatter, and then another shotgun blast. Bustle could see down the street at the corner of 152nd, street and Nestor two or more shadow figures and someone screaming out, "It's mad Pete Levi you don't f**k with me."

As the crowd began to scatter and run, Bustle tried to get up and run too, but the pain was too intense in both his legs to stand on his feet.

The pain was so intense that he fell back down. Not wanting to get shot again, he crawled underneath the nearest car, which was located in the driveway. At that time, fear began to set in, and thoughts were coming through his head. He feared that the shooter would find him under the car and shoot him again. So, he bravely crawled to the backyard. As much as he wanted to run, it just wasn't possible. Once he was in the backyard, he found a shed to hide from danger. When he reached the shed, he noticed that there was space between the shed and the fence that was filled with bricks, about 2 feet high. He dove on top of the bricks and stayed there quietly until the commotion died down praying that Pete and his crew wouldn't find him. After a while, he could hear the party-goers going around to check and see if anyone was hurt. Simon and Sykes were one of those searching and heard Bustle crying out for help. So, they went behind the shed, where they found Bustle lying there moaning in agony from the pain.

Simon said, "It's Bustle, he's been shot again!"

They carried him into the house and laid him on the kitchen floor. Someone else in the room saw what happened and called the paramedics. Bustle had been shot in both of his legs by a 20-gauge shotgun.

Buttback had also been hit by a stray pellet in one of her calves. Just before the paramedics arrived, Bustle began to go into shock from the loss of blood. When they got there, they put his legs into some type of device that inflated and put pressure on both legs. Soon after they rushed him off to the infamous Killer King Hospital.

Unlike his last visit from when he got shot, they put him to sleep to care for his gunshot wounds. When he woke up, he saw that one of his legs was elevated in the air with pins in it. He was told that his left leg was broken, and the other still had a few buck shots in it. After a few days in the hospital, they prepared his left leg for a cast. He had the usual visitors, such as his mom and few friends, to check on him. He also had detectives visit again to ask a question about that eventful night. They wanted to know who did this to him and if Bustle was willing to testify in court. The brave young man gave them the information they needed and was willing to testify in court. The stay in the hospital, this time, was short, and he only stayed for a few days.

Bustle had his cast on for about eight weeks and had to use crutches the whole time. After getting shot in the legs at a party while dancing in the street, Bustle found it hard to recover from that, mentally as well. He remembers going to another party in the neighborhood with his oldest brother Heavy and feeling really nervous. He broke out into a sweat; his legs were shaking; and he felt very uncomfortable like he was having an anxiety attack. This was unlike before when he was the life of the party and the first one to go out on the dance floor and dance, and he was always the first one to approach a girl and ask for a dance. This time, he was timid, withdrawn, and seem to be cowering in the corner. Even when one of his favorite songs was being played, *Aqua Boogie* by Parliament, it did not break him out of that shell. It wasn't until 1980 when the 'funk festival' concert at the LA Coliseum happened that Bustle felt a little more comfortable dancing. He was gifted tickets from his Aunt Annie who he just adored, maybe it was because he looks more like her than his own mom. She had the same bubbly eyes as him, same skin complexion, and when he looked at her hands and fingernails, seemed like they were so identical to his own.

Although she could be very stern and disciplinary, she was very generous. During Christmas time, some years when it may have been difficult and hard for his parents to provide any Christmas gifts for him, he remembers that he could always depend on his Aunt Annie to come over and bring them all some type of gifts. Well, it may not have been Christmas time, but when that concert came to town, she brought his brother Heavy and him a ticket, for them to go to that concert.

Chapter 11
New Man

In 1979, after getting shot for the second time, Bustle no longer thought he was too young to live a saved life. He decided to go back to church on a regular basis. So, Bustle went to service one night at Prayer Time Mission Church, his home church, when they were having a revival and Elder Marshall was the main speaker that night.

Elder Marshall was not only a preacher but also a pastor of his own church and a prophet of God. Most of his prophecies came true if not all of them. He may have had some faults, none that Bustle has ever seen or knew about, but just like everybody, we do the best; we can to serve God. Elder Marshall preached an anointed message so much so that Bustle, once again when the altar call was given by Elder Marshall, stood up and got in line to be prayed for. Now, Elder Marshall did not just pray for you, he asked questions.

Elder Marshall knowing that Bustle had accepted the Lord already asked him the question, "What is keeping you from serving God?"

Bustle began to ponder that question in his head, realized that it was a few things standing in his way. But, only mentioned one and failed to reveal the others and that one was that he had a problem getting into fights with a lot of people. So, Elder Marshall began to pray for Bustle so that the Lord would make a way so Bustle could not get into so many fights.

That summer, Bustle's pastor, pastor of Prayer Time Mission Church, decided to have a shut-in-fast in the church. A shut-in-fast is when you stay in the church for a length of time and you don't eat any food, only drink water occasionally, meditate on the Lord, pray, read your *Bible*, study, and stay for church services.

Now the pastor taught Bustle that you just don't have a fast just to have it, you should have a purpose for your fast. So, she told Bustle and the other members that participated in the fast to write down on a piece of paper their request that they have for the Lord to perform in their lives. So, Bustle wrote down that he wanted the Lord to bless him with new school clothes. He asked the Lord to bless him with a job, a moped, and he even asked the Lord to bless him to get married and have kids, especially a son. He also asked for wisdom and knowledge to understand the word of God; he asked the Lord to help him in school with his reading and learning. He asked to get closer to the Lord so that he could be able to do his will more.

They prayed; they studied; they fasted; they had church services. Day after day, night after night without eating, they prayed, studied, and had church services, for seven days straight. Although Bustle was physically weak, his spiritual man was very strong. On the last night of the fast, after church service, the pastor took them all out for dinner. They went to Norms restaurant, and Bustle had his favorite grilled ham and cheese sandwich with French fries and a sliced dill pickle on the side and his favorite drink, root beer soda.

Shortly after that, Elder Youngblood started a summer school *Bible* study class at Prayer Time Mission Church. Elder Youngblood was a 35-year-old man who was a musician, who preached, taught, and played guitar for the church. He lived in the church as he also was the caretaker of the church at the time he lived there. Bustle and a few of the members attended *Bible* school daily that summer for about 2 to 3 hours a day.

In addition to learning about *The Bible*, Elder Youngblood would tell stories about his life as a young man growing up serving God. Bustle remembers him telling him the stories about preaching and witnessing to his fellow classmates at Centennial High School in Compton, California. Preaching on the corner of streets in his neighborhood and also riding the bus preaching and witnessing to the bus riders. He told stories and talked with so much boldness and authority so much so that Bustle wanted to have that same power and authority in his life.

Summer was coming to an end, and the start of the 1979 school year was just a few days away. Bustle hadn't got any new school clothes yet. He wasn't too concerned because he could wear his older brother's hand-me-downs and any other kind of clothes, he could get his hands on. Most likely an old pair of jeans and a white T-shirt that didn't look so white anymore. So, he went about his day.

The next day, believe it or not, when Bustle came back in the house that day from playing outside, his mom had laid on his bed several pairs of new school clothes that his father paid for. She had told him that his dad had taken the last little bit of money that they had, went to the race track and won a lump sum of money. Bustle didn't care where his dad got the money from; all he knew was that his prayers were being answered.

Shortly after that, in 1979, Bustle was 15 years old when he got his first real job.

There was a burger stand on the corner of Compton Boulevard and Nester named Alex Burger stand. One day he and his mom were at Alex Burger stand, ordering a meal. The owner was talking to Bustle's mom to see if it was okay, if Bustle could work there.

She said, "Of course!"

Then he asked Bustle if he had a short-sleeve, white dress shirt. Whether he had one or not, he knew he could get one somehow.

He said, "Yes!"

So, the owner of the burger stand told him to come to the burger stand the next day at 4:00 PM with some work boots, a pair of jeans, and that white shirt. And to be clean-shaven; fingernails manicured and ready to work.

So, that day, Bustle did exactly what the owners said to do. He had all kinds of emotions going through his body as he showed up just a little bit before 4 o'clock. He was very happy and excited to have a job, yet nervous and unaware of what to expect as he reached the back door of the burger stand entrance. The man that Bustle knew as Alex met him at the back door, and the first thing, he did, was examined him from head to toe. He checked Bustle's hair to see if he needed to give him a hairnet. Well, Bustle always kept his hair cut very short anyway so there was no need for that, although he did give him a paper cap. He then made sure that his white short-sleeve shirt was clean and free of any debris.

And as he looked at his hands and fingernails, he began to explain to Bustle that it was very important to have good hygiene working in the food industry. Bustle remembers that to this day to keep his fingernails clean, trim, and very low. He made sure he had a belt on, to keep his jeans snug and tight around his waist. Last but not least, he made sure he had hard-toe nonslip-resistant work boots for safety in the kitchen.

Alex taught him how to use the grill for frying hamburger patties, bacon, ham and then showed him how to assemble a hamburger, how to use the deep fryer for French fries and other deep-fried foods. It was so much more different than cooking at home. At the midpoint of Bustle's shift, Alex told him he could have a lunch break. He told him he could fix any type of burger he wanted, a side order, and a drink and that he did not have to pay for it. That brought a smile to Bustle's face, not only was he going to get paid for cooking food, but he could also eat for free.

Bustle did not work every day; he only worked two, maybe three days a week.

Bustle was an opportunist. He decided that he needed to make more money. One of his not-so-close friends in the neighborhood was working at the dairy on the corner of Compton Boulevard and central, which was owned by another black businessman. His not-so-close friend told Bustle that he would clean the parking lot of that dairy for the owner twice a week for $25 each time, which came out to be $50 a week. Bustle remembers approaching the owner of the dairy and asking if he could work for him by cleaning his parking lot?

And the owner said, "I already have someone doing that for me."

Bustle being the person that he is said, "I would like to make you a proposition."

And the owner looked at Bustle with intrigue and smiled and said, "Come into my office, and we'll talk."

Bustle remembers the owner propping his legs up on his desk and saying, "Talk to me."

Bustle replied by saying, "I know he cleans your parking lot twice a week for $25 each time, coming out to be $50. I will clean your parking lot and over by the trash dumpster every day, including Sundays for $35 a week."

The owner looked at Bustle with such amazement; it seemed to be a much better offer than what he was getting already. It made it very hard for him to turn it down, so he accepted the offer. And Bustle knew that he had no chance of being a close friend of his not-so-close friend now.

Bustle was making a little bit of money now. He began to pay his tithes in church, 10% of his earnings. He also gave his parents some money. Whether he wanted to or not, he had to. Bustle had plenty of money left over to buy himself a moped. Oh, how happy Bustle was when he finally got his moped. He hadn't gotten it but for a day, when he went over to Beanie Boy's house and showed his moped off to him and his two sisters, Money Mae and Moran. When Beanie Boy's sisters asked if they could ride his moped, he hesitantly allowed them to ride it. The oldest one, Moran, was in the front operating the moped, while her sister Money Mae was sitting behind her. As Bustle and Beanie

Boy watch them ride off, swerving from side to side on the moped around the corner of 153rd, street, he anxiously waited for them to return.

When a few minutes pass by, he noticed both sisters from a distance walking, not riding the moped: one sister with the front wheel in her hand and the other sister pulling the rest of the moped behind her. Although it was a funny sight to see for everyone except for Bustle, he was crushed, almost in tears. They were all laughing as he grabbed both parts of his moped and went home.

In March 1980, Bustle and his parents moved out of the house on 153rd, street and Nester in Compton, California. And moved into a house on 106th, street and Vermont in Los Angeles, California. Bustle still having his job at Alex's burger stand and the cleanup job at the dairy in Compton, would ride his bicycle, that he had bought because he never got his moped fixed, all the way to Compton to work and to visit his friends in the neighborhood, and occasionally takes public transportation, the RTD bus.

One day when he was taking the bus to Compton, he remembered the stories of witnessing on the bus that Elder Youngblood told. So, he began to pray to God to give him the courage and boldness to be a witness for him on that bus. Bustle stood up and opened his *Bible* and went to Matthew 11:28, and read from it. "*Come unto me, all ye that labor and are heavy laden, and I will give you rest. Take my yoke upon you, and learn of me; for I am meek and lowly in heart: and ye shall find rest unto your souls. For my yoke is easy, and my burden is light.*"

Bustle began to tell the people that we're riding on the bus that if they were going through hard and difficult times in their lives, that they could come to God and God would ease those difficulties, and that if they got to know God they would realize he was a gentle and caring God, and that he would make things a lot more bearable for them in their lives. By getting to know him, they would also find out that by serving God, it was not going to be a difficult thing to do.

On his way back home, Bustle noticed a fried chicken fast food restaurant on the corner of Imperial and Vermont named Jim Dandy. Although Bustle had two part-time jobs, he decided to pay them a visit and see if they were hiring. To his surprise, when he asked the manager for an application, he gave him the application.

And as Bustle began to walk off with the application to take it home, the manager said, "No-no fill it out right now, right here."

Bustle, who could only read a little bit below his grade level, at the time, attempted to fill out the application, to the best of his ability. He turned in the application to the manager who began to read the application and performed an interview right there, on the spot, as the manager began to read Bustle's application everything seemed to be fine and in order until he reached a section of the application where it asked questions about your health. Bustle believed that the question was to be, "Do you have any wounds?" and he answered 'yes' to that question.

The manager pointed at the question and the answer and asked, "Do you have this?"

And Bustle said, "Yes!"

The manager pointing at the question and the answer and again said, "You have this?"

Bustle replied, "Yes, do you want to see?"

And the manager bewildered, quickly said, "No, no, no, I don't want to see! You have worms?"

Bustle hastily said, "No, no, no, I don't have worms! I thought it said wounds," and began to show the manager his gun-shot wound.

They both smiled and laughed, and the manager hired him on the spot and told him to come back the next day to be trained.

The Lord was blessing Bustle. Things on his list were coming true: he had gotten new school clothes; a job, not one but three jobs; the moped that he wanted; and he was able to get to know the Lord closer, through prayer and studying of his word. God truly was blessing him. Then one day while Bustle, his parents, his sister, and her five-month-old baby boy were eating breakfast at the kitchen table, a knock at the door; it was the Marshalls. To Bustle's surprise, they had a warrant to vacate the premises. The landlord was evicting them.

The Marshall said, "You have 10 minutes to grab your things and vacate the premises!"

Bustle's parents try to reason with the Marshall and discuss the matter.

But he replied, "There's nothing that I can do about it, I have to abide by the warrant you're wasting time, you only have 10 minutes!"

Bustle had not washed up or showered yet. He just grabbed some clothes and his TV and left the house. He got on the bus headed toward Compton hoping that he could stay at his friend Beanie Boy's house.

To the passengers on the bus, he may have looked like a teenage thug that just stole a TV set from somebody's house, at least that's the look that he was getting from them. It was such a horrible and embarrassing feeling of being evicted by the Marshalls that Bustle vowed that it would never happen to him again.

Upon arriving at Beanie Boy's house, Bustle made arrangements with his parents to stay in the church. Elder Youngblood had recently moved out so Bustle became the new caretaker. Living in the church made it possible for Bustle to get even more closer to God. Bustle would go to school work, all three jobs, and have time to pray, study, and meditate on God's word. This empowered and drove him to witness and preach on the corner of Central and Compton Boulevard.

As he was preaching and witnessing, he explained how good God is and how merciful God is. That he forgives sin and how God spared his life from being shot, not once but twice. And letting people know that it's never too late to come to God.

That Little Sally walked by. He had known her since she was a little girl and was a close friend of Little Piggy. She was about three years younger than Bustle and had gotten into drugs and turned to prostitution, working that same corner. He began to witness to her. Not by condemning her for what she was doing but by letting her know that God still loves her and wants the best for her. As she who was familiar with God's love being that she grew up in the church as well, began to tear up and repent there on the spot.

He also continued to witness on the RTD buses occasionally and at Compton High School where he attended. One day when Bustle was at school, the Lord led him to witness and preach to the students. The students would eat lunch outside, in an area that can be described as the town square. It was a wide-open area with cemented tables and benches. Now, earlier that day the principal allowed a man, who was a Muslim dressed in a suit with a bowtie, to pass out pamphlets that promoted his organization, on the campus. He was still there doing this lunch break, as Bustle began to read a verse out of *The Bible*. The Muslim man stood behind him as the crowd of students looked on.

You could hear sounds of whispering and shouting, with urgency and anticipation, to see what was going to happen between this Christian young man and the Muslim man. But to their disappointment, the Muslim man, although he may have disagreed with Bustle's Christian views, commended him, and said how proud he was that this young black man believed in something that was not detrimental to his peers. They shook hands and parted ways.

Now later that day, before school was dismissed, the word got out that a crew of guys from another neighborhood were going to fight with a crew of guys in Bustle's neighborhood: Simon, Sykes, Goofy, and AT. Normally, Bustle would have been part of this crew, but he hadn't fought anybody since he got prayed for by Elder Marshall. And oh! How he wanted to defend his friends in the neighborhood, yet he didn't want to break his vow to God.

So, after school, Bustle, his friends, and the other neighborhood crew rode the school bus home. When the bus driver approached the student drop-off point, one by one, they stepped off the bus, and before the bus pulled away, blows were being thrown. Simon was fighting one guy; Sykes another; Goofy was tussling with someone; and AT was even going at it. But no one touch Bustle, the power of that prayer followed him like a guardian angel.

Like the time when Bustle was riding his bike home from work, at Jim Dandy fast food restaurant, he had to ride past Hoover Street. When he preceded toward the corner traffic light, a group of Black gang members approached him and held onto his bicycle handlebars and said, "What set you from homie?" (Meaning: What gang are you in?)

Bustle, looking at their faces and demeanor, knew that no matter what he said, they were going to still jump him. Although he was scared, he thought to himself, "Well if I'm going to get beaten up, I might as well get beat for Christ's sake."

So, he answered, "I'm saved, I'm not in any gang. Would you guys like to accept Jesus Christ as your personal savior?"

Just like he thought it didn't matter what he said. The guy that was holding his handlebars said, "I don't want to hear any of that shit!" And as he reared back to throw a punch, they heard police sirens.

Bustle and the gang members were in the middle of traffic, and the light had turned green. So, the officer on the loudspeaker directed the young men to get out of the middle of the street and onto the sidewalk, as he began to verbally chastise them for holding up traffic. And another officer, understanding the situation at hand, allowed Bustle to ride off on his bike and they detained the gang members. Praise God! Guardian angels at work.

Yet another time in 1981, Bustle's sister lived at the Nickerson Gardens project in Watts. These projects were known for the Bounty Hunter Blood Gang. It was not a safe place to visit if you didn't have any affiliation with people that lived there. He went over to her house to get his hair done; she was applying a California Jheri curl to his hair; and she could not find her hair rollers and remembered that she lent them to her friend, who lives in a different building but in the same projects. So, she called her friend up and asked could she retrieve her hair rollers from her.

And she replied, "Yes, you can come over and pick them up now."

So, she told Bustle her friend's apartment number, which was just across the playground at that same Nickerson Gardens project. Bustle rushed out the door and began to run across that playground field. He soon realized that it was not a good idea as he began to hear someone whistle some type of gang signal.

And out of nowhere, it seemed, guys were coming out of their front doors, jumping over the back fences, coming from everywhere surrounding Bustle. They were all decked out in different types of apparel, but they all had on some red-colored clothes. Some of these guys had A-shirts, aka wife beaters, sagging pants, braided hair, some with barrettes. They had red bandana either around their heads, hanging out their pockets, or tied around their necks. Most, if not all of them, had some type of weapon in their hand.

Bustle was deep inside of their housing project. Unlike the time when he was rescued by the police, there would be no law-enforcement rescue this time. It may have been at least 15–20 gang members hovering around Bustle, with their eyes fixed on him. These were the meanest, rugged, toughest-looking gang members Bustle had ever seen! They were out for blood, no pun intended.

Bustle, trembling and terrified for his life, pointed across the playground and mumbled the words, "I was just going over to my friend's house."

When the smallest gang member out of the crowd approached Bustle, not knowing what to expect, Bustle braced himself for whatever may happen.

To his surprise, he wrapped his arms around him and said, "This is my friend calm down everybody!" as he led Bustle through the crowd of gang members.

Bustle, not recognizing him but with relief and joy began to give him dap (which means shake his hands), as they walked away together alone.

The small gang member confided in Bustle and said, "I know I don't know you, but I just didn't want to see it tonight, another massacre. I just didn't want to see that shit tonight!"

Bustle thanked him and went back to his sister's apartment and decided he was going to get those hair rollers another way. Guardian angels at work again. God made a way out of no way. Praise God!

Chapter 12
Drugs

Sometime in the year of 1975, Bustle and his family moved to the south central neighborhood, on 153rd, street, in Compton California, where he began to meet people in the neighborhood. The first person that Bustle met in the neighborhood was AT. His next-door neighbor, who was 12 years old. AT and Bustle became best friends. Bustle and AT had similar lives. They both had a younger sister; they were both the third boys born in their families. Even though they had similar family structures, AT's mother was very protective of him and his sister, and they were never allowed to go very far from home; however, Bustle was allowed to roam where ever he pleased.

Bustle also met Frank through AT. Frank was the only white boy Bustle knew in the neighborhood, who also lived on his street at the time. Although he was a little bit older than Bustle, maybe by 3 or 4 years, they were really close friends. Bustle was 11 years old when he first met Frank. Frank who was an only child, lived 3 houses down from AT, was very skilled at cinema and photography. Bustle and AT were playing in AT's backyard when Frank came over with his camera and started to film them playing around in the backyard.

AT and Bustle were into karate at the time and thought of a movie about a neighborhood bully that smoked cigarettes. Bustle was the bully, and AT was the victim. So, they began to ad lib. In the film, Bustle was beating up AT. But even at the age of 11, Bustle knew, although he was playing the part of the bully, he shouldn't win the fight. So, Bustle pretended to cough, and AT was able to get the upper hand and beat Bustle down. He used the fact that the bully smoked cigarettes, to show weakness and lose the fight.

Now, for Frank; he was very tech-savvy and extremely creative. Bustle was intrigued with Frank's creativity and how he could build props. He had all kinds of knives and swords; karate outfits, ninja outfits, he even crafted metal Japanese throwing weapons, like, Naruto Shuriken stars. He had them hanging all over his bedroom walls. Bustle and AT had Frank make them a pair of nunchakus that they absolutely loved.

Bustle met Frank's mother and his grandparents one day. Bustle saw how close of a family they were and admired that. Frank also introduced Bustle to classical music, something that Bustle was very unfamiliar with but began to enjoy.

Frank was also close with AT's oldest brother Rabbit. Rabbit was a black belt in karate, and Frank was a brown belt at the time. Because of Rabbit's known skill and knowledge in karate, gang members revered him and would not challenge his abilities, for it just took for him to demonstrate his abilities one time. As he was known to have beaten up three gang members at once. Rabbit would train

Bustle and AT in his backyard, of course, because AT couldn't go anywhere.

Frank and Rabbit were very close in age, and they hung out a lot, so both Rabbit and Frank would teach them quite often. Rabbit was mostly known for his kicking ability, and Frank for his punching ability. Rabbit would teach them all types of ways to defeat their opponents by low kicks and high kicks. One of the low kicks that Bustle remembers getting taught was by kicking an opponent in the kneecap. Now, Bustle was taught only to use this technique in an emergency. Now, Bustle was not only learning how to give blows but how to block blows as well.

In the year 1977, when the series *Roots* was first televised, it ruffled feathers in the neighborhood. Bustle went to school the next day and vividly remembers a white kid getting beat up just simply because he was white. After witnessing this, Bustle immediately feared for his friend Frank. Bustle had grown very close to Frank and was willing to defend his close friend at all costs.

Now, the late '70s hit, drugs are on the rise more than ever. Bustle was still friends with Frank but found himself more distant from him. Bustle would notice Frank walking around the neighborhood from time to time with a bag. Frank who was once a husky overweight teenager, who then became trimmed up muscular and had an athletic body because of his martial art training, now was a skinny dried up skeleton of a man.

Bustle would see that Frank was actually huffing aka sniffing paint out of the bag. Now, that intelligent, bright, creative person was now altered and the Frank that Bustle knew seemed to be only a lifeless shadow. Bustle would go to Frank and plead with him to stop the drugs and to see the damage he had done to himself. Bustle had hoped that he could get through to him, but every time he finished talking to him, Frank would look at Bustle and then his bag of paint, take a huff, and continue on down the street as though Bustle had said nothing to him.

As Bustle reflected on these events, he thought to himself there had to be a reason for Frank to want to self-destruct. After a while of thinking Bustle realized that Frank's grandparents had passed away. Remembering how close of a family they were, Bustle realized that Frank was trying to numb his pain, through drugs or any way he could.

During the same time, Rabbit had a girlfriend/fiancé, and they had a baby. They were also known for doing drugs at this time even though they had the baby. One day, they were using heavy drugs and had a bad trip; they ended up boiling the baby in a pot on the stove. Rabbit's mom came home to find the horrifying scene of Rabbit and his girlfriend smashed and stupefied on the couch while their precious baby laid boiling in a pot. She immediately called the police, and they took Rabbit and his girlfriend to jail.

Bustle was in shock, especially knowing that Rabbit and Frank had been into extreme fitness and healthy living. Little did Bustle know that this was only the beginning of a list of things to come.

The era of crack was now happening, and most of the friends that Bustle grew up with, slowly but surely began to get into the drug scene. In the year 1980, one of Bustle's friends, Lil J, only 13 years old, followed in the path of an older brother by starting to sell crack on the corner. Lil J found himself selling crack on the corner of a rival gang.

To teach him a lesson, they broke a bottle and with the sharp edges of the top broken part of the bottle, placed it tightly on his face, around his lips, and turned violently ripping off his lips. After this, Lil J was never heard from or seen again that Bustle knew of. But that didn't deter other kids in the neighborhood from selling drugs.

One day a middle-aged woman drove up to the corner, where two brothers and their crew were selling crack. She looked to be harmless, almost as though she could be a member of a church. One of these two brothers approached the car on the passenger side to give her the drugs. As he put his arm through the window, she rolled the window up trapping his arm, and suddenly drove off, sporadically, ramming him into parked cars or whatever she could to free him from her vehicle. Bustle witnessed the brother run to where his brother's body had fallen and saw him strip the brother of all drugs and money, only to run off and leave him, not knowing if his brother was dead or alive.

Bustle also had a close friend whose name was Kurt. Kurt lived around the corner from Bustle; they both were about 16 years old at this time. They've been friends for a while. They went to Compton High School, where they attended and tried out for the high school football team together along with Beanie Boy. After school, they lifted weights and train together. Kurt started going with Beanie Boy and Bustle to the Tuesday night evangelistic services. Soon after, Kurt devoted his life to Christ. So, in addition to training for football tryouts, together they would often read and study *The Bible* as well.

Kurt was the youngest child in his immediate family. He had a much older sister who started having kids when he was just a toddler. This means, at 16 years old, he had a 13-year-old nephew. Being that he was a devoted Christian now, he tried to look out for his nephew and keep him out of trouble.

There was another 13-year-old kid, who live next door to Beanie Boy who had joined a notorious known gang, outside of the neighborhood. Now, it was known that Kurt's nephew would often hang around this kid. This young gangbanger was also known for robbing, killing, and selling drugs. Kurt not wanting his nephew around this kid decided that he would come between them because he knew that it would lead to nothing but trouble if he did not intervene.

So, one day when Kurt, Bustle, and Beanie Boy were coming home from football tryouts, Kurt notices the young gangbanger talking to his nephew. So, they all walked up toward them and Kurt began to demand that they stay away from each other. He orders his nephew to go home and tells the kid. "I better not ever see you talking or hanging around my nephew again!"

The next day Bustle found out that Kurt had been shot and killed by his own nephew. The word in the neighborhood was that the same young thug that Kurt confronted, whose name was Ulysses, gave Kurt's nephew a gun and ordered him to shoot and kill Kurt if he wanted to stay in the gang that they were in.

Little Piggy and a few other neighborhood girls had also started to use drugs. Unfortunately, to support their habit they became prostitutes. One of those young ladies was Little Sally, the one that Bustle witness on the corner of Central and Compton Boulevard. She went with a 'John', and the next day, they found her dead.

Drugs began to affect almost everyone in the community, whether they were taking them or being affected by someone who was taking them. Drugs are extremely powerful and take over your life no matter what you have or do not have; all the riches in the world cannot save you from the evil grip that drugs can hold on a person. For example, Little Piggy had won the lotto not once but twice. She had won over million-plus dollars, but drugs were too great of a temptation, in her life for her to utilize that money for the right and proper things in life. Drugs enabled her to evaporate that money in less than a year.

Bustle's best friend Beanie Boy was also struggling and fell into drug addiction as well. Beanie Boy's addiction was so deep that he began to commit robberies with the help of one of his sisters. His sister would be the seductive bait; after the victim was lured into a location, Beanie Boy would rob them. One day, Beanie Boy and an older gangster, we call him Sleepy, from the neighborhood, which so happens to be the uncle of the kid that told Kurt's nephew to shoot him, decided to rob a jogger in the park. After beating up the jogger and taking his money, they divided the bounty of $1.75; this was the robbery that ultimately got them caught and sentenced to 5 years in prison.

Down through the years, even Bustle's brother Heavy fell victim to drugs. This hit Bustle the hardest. Bustle had a code not to deal with anybody that was using drugs because he knew that there was nothing that he could do for them to help them. Seeing his brother, who was a big, strong black man that he looked up to, who protected him from danger so many times in his life being subdued by drugs, hurt Bustle to the core.

You could no longer call him Heavy. Drugs had dried up his brother to a point that he had to walk with the cane. This time, Bustle ignored his code. He tried with all his might to convince his brother not to take drugs, up until the point where he would physically grab him, shake him, hit him trying to force him not to go out in the streets and buy drugs.

I can go on and on telling you the many different scenarios and situations of drug abuse that Bustle had seen in his lifetime. Unfortunately, this book would not be able to hold all of them. So, I am just going to say once again, drugs are extremely powerful; avoid them at all costs and if you are involved with drugs, seek help immediately, through your clergymen or public assistance. God will make a way. Trust him!

Chapter 13
Being a Young Strong Blackman

It's March 1981; Bustle was 16 years old, lived in the church, and he was going to Compton High School practically every day. It was there where he begins to get As, Bs, and Cs on his report card when in the past he would receive Cs, Ds, and Fs. He takes two future work job proposal tests that are being given at his school: one for the post office and the other for Northrop Aircraft Facility, which they will mail him the results to home.

He stays in school only until noon because he uses two of the three jobs he had for elective classes. He takes driver's educational classes so that he can get his license before he turned 18. At that age, Bustle felt that getting his license early would help him accomplish the things he needed to do to become a man.

After getting his permit, his oldest brother Heavy begins teaching him how to drive. They were using their uncle's 1971 powder-blue Volkswagen beetle for Bustle to learn how to drive with. His brother told him, "If you learn how to drive with a stick, there will be no problem for you to drive an automatic."

His brother was very patient with him while he was teaching him how to drive. Their uncle allowed them to use his car only if Bustle, since he was working, would pay for his little sister to get contact lenses. Well, even if Bustle had not been allowed to use his car, he had so much respect for his uncle that he would've done whatever his uncle said anyway, so that seemed like a fair deal.

Soon after receiving his license, Bustle had his eye on a Canary yellow-colored 1971 Chevrolet Vega Notchback Sedan, which he had seen for sale in someone's yard on his way home from school for only $500. Bustle had saved up enough money beforehand and decided to purchase that vehicle even though friends and family would criticize him for buying a car with a so-called aluminum motor. Bustle adored that car. As he drove up and down the street, little kids would wave and cheer as he drove by like he was driving a racecar.

His brother Pookie found out and asked him could he use his car that same day he bought it.

Bustle was still intimidated by his older brother Pookie and said, "I have to go to work right now."

And Pookie replied, "I can drop you off at work and pick you up when your shift ends at 10 PM."

Well, his brother Pookie dropped him off at Jim Dandy's, where he worked and drove off, with the music blasting out of the roll-down windows. At 10 PM, Bustle was off work, but there was no sign of his brother Pookie outside to pick him up. Well, the manager waited with Bustle for about 25 minutes, no Pookie. So, the manager said, "I can give you a ride home if you'd like."

Bustle, sad and disappointed that his brother did not keep his word, excepted the ride home from his manager.

All through that night, no Pookie. The next day, he could hear his car coming up the street, music blasting, and because of that aluminum motor, it sounded like a revved-up racecar. Yes, it was his brother Pookie coming down the street, but to his surprise, Pookie drove right past the church where Bustle was standing and went down the street. Now, Bustle was no longer intimidated by his brother but now furious with him and frustrated with himself for allowing his brother to do him like this.

It was approaching the time for Bustle to be at work, and he was standing outside in front of the church about to walk down the street and catch the bus to work when, finally his brother drove by, and this time, stopped in front of him. At first glance at his car, Bustle noticed that his passenger side headlight was missing and a big dent on that same side. His brother, exiting the car and holding the headlight in his hands, apologized saying, "I'm sorry. I wrecked your car."

Although Bustle was upset with his brother, he was not going to retaliate, in any way. He held all that frustration inside of himself, but he also realized that he would never lend his brother anything again, at least for the moment.

Bustle always had a thing for Beanie Boy's younger sister Money Mae, but she was only 15 years old, and he was 17 years old, and even though he was living in the church, which is located behind their house, her parents still did not allow her to have a courtship with anybody, even Bustle. So, Bustle had his eyes on another young lady named Loretta.

She was the daughter of Beanie Boy's father's friend, who sang in a gospel group with him. She was the same age as Bustle. The first time he saw her was in church during a gospel concert. She was singing with her sisters as a group. Bustle compared them to the Clark Sisters. She also attended Compton High School along with Bustle and had at least one class period with her. Her younger sister Teresa, who was 14 years old, had a crush on Beanie Boy, who of course was 16 years old, and he had a crush on her as well.

So, on one day, Beanie Boy asked Bustle to drive him over to Teresa's house. Bustle, hoping that Loretta would be home as well, decided to take him over there hoping for a chance to woo her. To his delight, Loretta was home with Teresa and one of their other sisters Cora. While they were talking and reminiscing all night in the kitchen the conversation of prom night came up. At last, Bustle saw his chance and asked if could he take Loretta to the prom. She accepted, and they made plans to go shopping for a prom dress and a suit for Bustle.

The next day, instead of going to the mall, they went to the Huntington Park shopping strip, which is similar to a shopping mall, but it's outdoors down a long boulevard street. As Bustle began to romance her, he found himself not only buying her a Prom dress but several other outfits as well. And then they walked past a jewelry shop and somehow Bustle found himself inside the jewelry shop with her. They were looking at all the jewelry that they had displayed in the glass cases, all around the shop, and came across a promise ring that Loretta was just absolutely thrilled about.

She asked Bustle, "What do you think about this ring?"

And Bustle replied, "It's very nice. I'll get it for you if you can keep the promise."

Well, that made Loretta even more excited. So, she said, "Yes, of course, and since we're here, we might as well get the wedding rings!"

That kind of surprised Bustle, but he was in agreement. They left the promise ring there and begin to pick out matching wedding bands and an engagement ring. After that, they decided to inform their respective parents about their decision to get married. They first went to Bustle's parents' apartment and announced that they were getting married.

Upon hearing this announcement, Bustle's mom smiled and said, "Congratulations, I am very happy for the both of you!" But his dad, looking at the both of them, shook his head back-and-forth, smiled, and continue looking at whatever television show that he was watching.

So, when Bustle mustered up enough nerve to ask her parents, he did, by asking for their permission to marry their daughter. Waiting in anticipation for their response or answer was happily surprised to hear them say, "Yes!"

They were very happy as well, and her sisters were there also and began to say, "So when are you guys getting married? Right away? Tomorrow?"

Although Bustle was ready as soon as possible, he simply said, "It's up to Loretta, whenever she wants to."

She thought about it for a little while and said, "We're going to set it a year from now."

Now Loretta had told Bustle that although they were engaged, she did not want to have intercourse until they got married. She explained that with her previous boyfriend, having sex messed up their relationship, and she didn't want to have the same results happen to their relationship. So, Bustle sadly abided by her wishes.

But one day, about a month later, when she was babysitting her niece and nephew for her oldest sister and husband at their house overnight, she called Bustle to come over and spend some time with her. When the kids fell asleep, she put them to bed, and while Bustle was in the living room watching TV, she came into the room with a blanket, and they cuddled on the couch.

Normally, Bustle would seize this opportunity to make advances on her, but he truly cared for Loretta and did not want to ruin his relationship with her. He did not attempt in any way to make any sexual advances on her. They fell asleep in each other's arms, and on the next morning, just before he left for work, she made it known to him that she desperately wanted to have sex that night.

He shouted out, "Me too, so can we do it tonight?"

She said, "No, we're going to keep our arrangement just the way it is and wait till we get married."

Boy did that make him feel terrible, and he thought to himself, "I messed up and missed out on a great opportunity."

On his way to work, he got pulled over by the police. Now, remember Bustle is a young teenage black man, driving a car with his music playing loud during a time when the president has called war on drugs and is now being pulled over by LAPD. Also, keep in mind Bustle is sexually frustrated, and he has to keep his composure while dealing with the police. Both officers, with their guns, pointed at Bustle car and told him, "Turn off your vehicle, step out of the car, lay flat on the ground with your arms spread out to the side and your feet spread apart!"

Bustle complies with their demands and gets out of the car. One officer rushes toward him, places his knee on his back, and applies pressure while grabbing his arms, one at a time, behind his back and handcuffs him.

Then the officer stands up while pulling Bustle to his feet, slamming him on the hot hood of his car, and pressing his face down even more on the hood. Bustle tries to resist the urge to draw back from the heat of the car and the pain he is going through endorse it as the officer begins to ask him, as he is searching him, "Do you have any weapons on you? Do you have any sharp objects that will pierce my skin like a syringe or knife?"

Bustle quickly says, "No!" in agony. They run his plates and driver's license number and find that he has no priors, releases him with a ticket for touching the yellow line with his tire while driving on the road.

Now, this is one ticket out of three that Bustle has received before he even turns 18 years old. The first one seemed to Bustle to be like a routine stop. The police officer pulled Bustle over, approached the vehicle, asked Bustle for his driver's license and registration card, and said, "Do you know why I pulled you over?"

And Bustle answered, "No, I'm not sure why."

The office replied, "Your passenger headlight is out."

Then the officer ran his license and gave him a fix-it ticket and told him to have a nice day and left. But the third time was neither like the first or the second time. It was late at night; Bustle was coming from work going home, on a dark street somewhere in LA and two white police officers pulled him over and, on their loudspeaker, told him, "Exit the vehicle and slowly walk to the back of your car!"

Again, Bustle complied with their demands. The police officers with their guns drawn and pointed at him, one at a time, approach Bustle. One of the officers holstered his weapon and began to handcuff Bustle. Then they search him and pulled out his wallet and his driver's license and placed him on the curve. They begin to tell him that they pulled him over because he fit the description of a suspect who they were looking for.

Now, Bustle didn't know exactly what was going on with one of the police officers, but he had a real mean and nasty attitude toward Bustle who had done nothing to him. The officer may have had a bad day at home or before he came to work or while he was at work earlier that day. Bustle did not know, but it seemed that whatever may have happened to him or how he felt about something, the officer directed all of his frustration and anger toward Bustle who he just met for the first time.

Looking at Bustle with rage and disdain for him, he grabbed Bustle and shoved him into the backseat of their patrol car and began to have a conversation with his partner. They were discussing what they should do to him saying, "We could take him down that alley and kill him and leave him there like we did that other piece of shit."

Bustle, with his head down not begging for his life or anything, said nothing the whole time they were talking. But it seemed like the other officer had some compassion for Bustle and said, "We don't really have to do that to him he seems like a nice young man and has no priors."

Then he turned and looked at Bustle and said, "What are you doing out here late at night?"

Bustle answered, "I just got off work, and I was going home."

So the officers let him off with a warning saying, "If I ever catch you out here in the streets committing some type of crime, we're not going to arrest you, we're going to do exactly what we said we were going to do to you, so stay out of trouble."

They unhandcuffed him and let him go. Bustle did not know if they were serious or just playing with him; he did not want to find out either way. I'm not saying that all police officers are like this, but as a black person, let alone a black young man, when you get confronted by law enforcement, it's like playing Russian roulette; you don't know if this time the police officer is going to kill you or not.

Two months passed and Bustle gets a letter in the mail, it's from the Postmaster at the post office in Downey California. It states that he has a job interview for a Clerk Carrier position at that post office and informed him to bring the necessary paperwork and a copy of his DMV driver's license record for the past three years.

Bustle gets all of those items ready and on the day of the interview talks with the Postmaster. Just like the Jim Dandy interview with the manager, the Postmaster goes over all the paperwork, and everything seems to be in order until he gets to the DMV driver's license record report and notices that Bustle has three violations.

He questions Bustle about that, and he replied, "Yes, I had three tickets, but I paid them all off. I don't owe anything now."

Bustle was unaware at that time that paying the fines on your tickets does not make them go away. They stay on your record pretty much forever but cannot be used against you after three years have passed. The Postmaster informs Bustle that he cannot offer him the position and explains to him why not.

He says, "Because you have these three violations, our company cannot ensure you, if there were just one you would have a chance, but because you have these three violations, I'm sorry I cannot offer you the job."

Unlike the Jim Dandy job interview, Bustle could not explain his way out of this, sadly he thanked the Postmaster and leaf.

One week later, Bustle is washing his car in front of the church where he lives.

Money Mae offers to help him wash his car; still attracted to her, he allows her to help. They're having a nice time talking, smiling, and splashing water and soap on each other as they washed his car. When they finished washing the car, she asked him, "I'm going over to my sister's house. Can you take me?"

Bustle answered, "Yes, of course; hop in the car."

On the way over, he stopped at a local fast-food restaurant, and they had lunch. Now, the reason why she was going over to her sister's house was to babysit her sister's kids, so when they got there; somehow they decided to all go to the park. Bustle drove them to the local park, and while the kids were playing, Bustle and Money Mae set on the grass underneath a shady tree and talk about when they were a little bit younger. They had a really nice time that day.

But the next day, Bustle took his fiancé Loretta to Santa Monica Pier where they had fun also playing games, winning prizes, and taking pictures. He felt guilty after spending so much time with Money Mae the day before, decided that he would tell his fiancé Loretta that he spent the other day with Money Mae, but nothing happened, he began to explain.

She said, "I appreciate your honesty, but I'm a little hurt; it's all good; see you tomorrow."

Bustle thinking everything's fine replied, "Okay, I'll get these pictures developed, and then I'll come over and give them to you when they're ready; see you later."

Later that day, Bustle goes over to his parents' place where they now live in an apartment in Long Beach, California. When he gets there, he notices that his mom is unresponsive but is still moving around mumbling something and seems to be in some discomfort. Bustle, not knowing where his dad is, calls 911 and explains to the dispatcher the circumstances that are happening to his mom.

They tell Bustle, "The paramedics are on the way, stay on the phone with me till they get there."

Bustle was very concerned. He was not sure if she was having a nervous breakdown or just in serious physical pain. He felt helpless, even though the 911 dispatcher was on the phone with him, trying to calm him down and guide him through the necessary steps to care for his mother, he still did not want to see her in so much pain. When the paramedics arrived, they assess the situation, then took her to the hospital.

Bustle began to pray and said, "Lord do not let anything happen to my mama. Protect her on every side!" Then immediately thought, "I have to get to my Pastor, (The woman of God which is Beanie Boy's mother) quickly. I need her to pray for my mom!"

Bustle knew that she was a devoted God-fearing, Holy Ghost shouting, anointed woman of God and when she prayed for you miracles would occur in your life. He drove over to her house as fast as he could trying to obey all traffic laws. When he got there and entered the house, she was sitting down on the couch in the living room talking with some of her church member friends. Bustle rudely interrupted their conversation and said, "My mom is sick we have to pray for her!"

The woman of God stopped him in his tracks and put him in his place said, "You don't interrupt me when I'm having a conversation with my friends, have you prayed already?"

Bustle said, "Yes!"

And She replied, "Well, wait until I finish my conversation with my friends, then I'll pray with you for your mother if you still want me to."

Bustle couldn't believe that she was not feeling the same way he was about the situation. To him, he thought he was the only one that felt that this was a serious and desperate situation that needed to be attended to immediately. After she prayed with him for his mom, she lets him know that he did not have to be in a rush or panic.

She said, "If you're in a personal relationship with God on a daily basis, all you have to do is speak the word, and God will hear you wherever you are."

Well, that lesson taught Bustle a lot. He realized she was right, and it taught him to put his trust more in God than in any one person. Oh! he still reverenced and respected his pastor and showed her honor, always. But he realized that God was performing all the miracles in his life through her. And that no matter where he was or who was with him, as long as he abided in God's will, he could get in contact with him at any time. And that's all that matters.

Bustle went to the hospital to find out what was wrong with his mother. When he got there, he found out that she was in surgery. The doctor said she had spinal meningitis, (inflammation of the brain and spinal cord membranes typically caused by an infection, if not treated can cause death in 24 hours) and that they had to operate on her by draining fluid from her forehead. He also said, "I had to put her in an induced coma, and you're lucky that we got to her in time. Hopefully, she'll be okay, and only have a little brain damage that causes slow motor skills."

Bustle was calm yet concerned but did not worry for he had prayed already for his mom and left it in God's hands.

His Aunt Annie was in the hospital as well, and he went to go visit her. He didn't know exactly what was wrong with her, but she was a heavy smoker like his mom. He believes she was having some respiratory problems but he was not sure. So much was happening at one time, his memory was a little foggy. Seeing her lying there in that hospital bed so weak and helpless made him very sad, when to him she was the strongest black woman that he had ever known. This made it hard for him to bear. Of course, Bustle thought his mother was one of the toughest women he knew, but his Aunt Annie was the only woman that his mother listened to and obeyed. So, seeing her like that grieved him.

The next day when he went over to visit his fiancé Loretta to give her the film that he had gotten developed, she met him at the door and said, "We need to talk."

So, she let him in the house, and they sat down on the couch in the living room. She simply said, "I think we need to call off the wedding." She paused and looked at him waiting for his response. Now keep in mind, Bustle was so infatuated with this young lady that he thought he was the luckiest man in the world just to have her as a girlfriend let alone his fiancé.

This made him not want to say or do anything that might jeopardize his relationship with her. He simply said, "Okay."

Then she said, "Well, I don't think we should be boyfriend and girlfriend anymore either." Even though the very thing that Bustle was afraid of was happening to him at that moment, he still did not want to say or do anything that would displease her.

Again, he simply said, "Okay."

Then Loretta stood and finally said, "And I don't think you should come over here to see me anymore."

That hit Bustle like a ton of bricks, but he did not show it. He did not want to let her know that she had just crushed his heart. He stood up, handed her the developed pictures, said, "Okay," walked out the door, got in his car, and could no longer hold back the tears and started crying.

He thought to himself, "What did I do wrong? Was it because I didn't have sex with her that night when she was babysitting her niece and nephew? Or it could have been the other day when I told her about me spending time with Money Mae. Maybe it's my gunshot wound? She probably doesn't like to be with somebody that has an injury like mine. Or, she did say that I had bad breath, but I'm trying to solve that by brushing my teeth every day. I even buy mints and use them all the time or maybe it's my teeth, I have this big gap in the front of my mouth."

Bustle could not pinpoint exactly what it was; all he knew was that she didn't want to see him anymore, and that's all that matters. He didn't want to beg her to be with him so he drove off and went home.

The next day while Bustle was at the hospital visiting his mom, he was informed that his Aunt Annie died earlier that day. Bustle felt guilty and thought to himself, "Have I spent too much time thinking about my own problems that I have neglected to earnestly pray for my aunt?" So many emotions were going back-and-forth through his mind that he had to go home and pray and get some rest.

Well, that did not last very long because he got a phone call, it was Loretta's mom on the other end of the line, she said, "What in the world is going on between you and Loretta?"

Bustle answered, "She called off the wedding and said that she didn't want to see me anymore."

Her mother replied, "Well she's over here crying her little heart out for you!"

Then Bustle said, "I'll be right over to talk to her!"

When he got there Loretta's mom let him in the house and said, "She's in the bathroom; it's okay, you can go in and talk to her there."

Bustle entered the bathroom and looked at Loretta, who did not appear to look like someone who was crying, was applying makeup to her face. Perhaps to cover up the fact that she had been crying.

He asked her, "What's wrong? Why were you crying? Didn't you break up with me?"

She answered as she was looking into the mirror, applying the makeup around her eyes, "Yes I did. I did that because I wanted you to fight for me. When we first got together you pursued me, it made me feel special. So, I wanted to feel that again. I wanted you to fight for this relationship."

Then Bustle said, "Okay, Okay! I can do that!"

She stopped him from talking and said, "No, it's too late now; it's not the same."

Bustle didn't want to argue with her, and he sadly said, "Okay," and left again.

Bustle drove home to the church where he was still living. When he got there, he noticed two bicycles by the back porch of the front house. Instead of going into the church where he was staying, he went to the iron security back door and knocked on the door. Well, no one came to the door soon enough for him. He immediately began to bang harder on the door. Moran answered the door and said, "What do you want, Bustle? Is Money Mae here?"

She replied, "What do you want with her?"

He said, "I want to talk to her."

She unlocked and open the door to let Bustle inside. He walked through and immediately walked toward the living room where he saw Greg, who he knew was Moran's boyfriend and Money Mae sitting on the couch, next to some guy that he had never seen before cuddled up with her arms wrapped around him. Not thinking, Bustle drove right on top of the guy and told him, "Get your hands off of her!"

Moran, Greg, and Money Mae pulled Bustle off the guy and dragged him out the door and locked the door behind them. Bustle was outraged. He began to bang on the iron door and screamed out Money Mae's name saying, "Can I talk to you, Money Mae? Please come and talk to me!"

Moran began to tell him, "Get away from the door and go home; she doesn't want to talk to you!"

He began to beg and said, "Please, Money Mae, please come and talk to me!"

Moran said, "If I let her come talk to you, will you leave after that?"

He answered, "Yes, I will!"

So, Money Mae came to the locked iron security door with Bustle on the other side.

He said, "Do you want to be with me?"

And she said, "I thought you supposed to be engaged to Loretta?"

He answered, "We're not engaged anymore; we're not getting married. So, do you want to be with me?"

Moran said, "No, she doesn't want to be with you!"

And Bustle replied, "I want to hear it from her mouth" (referring to Money Mae's mouth).

Bustle looked into Money Mae's eyes and asked, "Do you want to be with me?"

She looked at Moran, then at Bustle, and then at the floor. Then said, "No, I don't want to be with you."

Bustle seem to be out of control; he wanted to fight. He started calling both of the young men out to fight, taunting them by saying, "Are you guys too scared to come out and fight me? Are you chicken?"

He got no reaction out of them, seeing their bicycles there he began to pick them up one at a time and throw them to see if that would make them come out and fight. Although they may have wanted to go out and fight with Bustle and beat him to a pulp, Moran and Money Mae would not let them go outside to fight him. That prayer was still with Bustle. His Guardian Angels, despite him wanting to fight, were still there to keep God's word in full. God is so merciful.

Moran and Money Mae's parents drove up and pulled into the driveway. Bustle seeing them thought to himself, "Now they're going to get it, as soon as their parents find out that they got two boys in the house with them alone, while they're gone, boy oh boy are they going to be sorry, and I'm the one that's going to let them know."

Bustle ran up to the car as they were exiting. In a panic, as he was gasping for breath because of his antics that he just displayed and said, "Moran and Money Mae have two boys in the house with them!"

And their mother, the woman of God said, "I know, they were here when we left and what are you doing here, you need to go somewhere."

The disappointment in Bustle's heart was overwhelming to him. He did not expect to hear that from her; he felt like he was a stranger to them. Bustle walked to where his car was parked on Nestor street between 152nd, and 153rd, facing toward 153rd, street. So, let me set up the demographics of Bustle's neighborhood. They lived in (Taco Flats, known for the Latino infamous 1 5 5 gang) between Compton Boulevard Central Avenue, Tajauta Avenue, and 155th, street and between those four cross streets was 151st, 152nd, 153rd, and 154th, street and Nestor ran right through, the middle of them. But when you got to 155th, street there was a brick wall at the end of Nestor street, that was graffitied up with the 1 5 5 gang logos and all their tags.

While Bustle sat in his car, facing that brick wall at a distance, he was mad, angry, and confused. He thought to himself, "After all of this time, now she finally lets Money Mae have a boyfriend."

Bustle screamed and cried out those thoughts as he hit the turning wheel of his car, "Now she can have a boyfriend!" he said to himself.

He started thinking more, "Loretta doesn't want me; Money Mae has a new boyfriend and doesn't want me either. My mom is in the hospital in a coma, and my Aunt Annie is dead and gone now. I didn't get the post office job because I got those tickets from those police officers that didn't care about me. My life doesn't matter anymore."

All of these thoughts went back and forth through Bustle's head as he looked at the brick wall, down that street, at the end of the corner. He continued thinking, "I can end it all, no more pain, no more going through things like trying to survive every day. I can drive this car right down the street as fast as I can right into that wall and end it all; no one cares about me anyway; my life doesn't matter to anybody."

Bustle started the engine on his car and, while still in the parked position, stepped on the gas pedal revving his motor engine higher and higher. And before he could do anything (it seemed similar too but not exactly like on TV when a little red-dressed-up devil pops up on the left side of your ear telling you negative things that then on the right side of your ear a little angel dressed in white pops up and begins to tell you positive things) so before Bustle could react to those negative thoughts, he began to think, "I was there lying on that kitchen floor dying asking God to give me another chance and God spared my life, and when I prayed for school clothes, a moped, a job, and not to be in any more fights, God blessed me with all of those things. God cares about me I matter to him. And even though one of those police officers seemed like he didn't care about me at all, the other one did care about me."

So, Bustle decided that God spared his life for a reason and a purpose that it wouldn't be right to end his life for nothing; he had to be strong. Bustle felt ashamed about just having the thought of suicide; to him, suicide showed a sign of weakness. But to a young black man suicide is a thought that plagues him on a daily basis; whether it's conscious or subconscious, dealing with the circumstances surrounding you in this concrete jungle we call South Central LA is a daily task. Some people succumb to it, not by literally committing suicide but by a destructive life pattern. Like using or selling drugs, joining a gang, committing the armed robbery, and the list goes on and on. Just like Ice Cube's song, *How to survive in South Central*! It was a good illustration of how things were in that era. Well, for Bustle, how to survive was to have the Lord Jesus Christ in his life, that's how he survived. The word says in Ephesians, 6:10–18:

Finally, my brethren, be strong in the Lord, and in the power of his might. Put on the whole armor of God, that ye may be able to stand against the wiles of the devil. For we wrestle not against flesh and blood but against principalities, against powers, against the rulers of the darkness of this world, against spiritual wickedness in high places. Wherefore take unto you the whole armor of God, that ye may be able to withstand in the evil day, and having done all, to stand. Stand therefore, having your loins girt about with truth, and having on the breastplate of righteousness; And your feet shod with the preparation of the gospel of peace; Above all, taking the shield of faith, wherewith ye shall be able to quench all the fiery darts of the wicked. And take the helmet of salvation, and the sword of the Spirit, which is the word of God: Prayer and supplication in the Spirit, and watching thereunto with all perseverance and supplication for all saints.

That's how to survive, if you take these eight verses of *The Bible* and apply them to your life, God will make a way. So, Bustle turned off his car, went into the church, prayed, and went to sleep.

The next morning, he decided that he wasn't going to give up; instead of choosing to fight for Loretta, he fought for Money Mae. With the ring in his hand, he went to the front house to speak to Money Mae alone in her bedroom, but Moran was there in the hallway, and she said to him, "What are you going to do with that ring? You going to ask Money Mae to marry you now?"

He looked at her and smiled; then he walked into the bedroom up to Money Mae and said, "I can't live without you; will you be my wife?"

She smiled, giggled a little, and said, "Yes, I will."

Moran was eavesdropping from the hallway and heard what they said to each other and ran into the bedroom where they were in front of Money Mae, and they both began to hug each other, jumping up and down screaming, "Yay!"

Then Moran said, "Are you guys going to ask mom and dad if it's okay with them if you guys get married?"

Money Mae looked at Bustle and said, "He's going to have to ask."

Bustle replied, "I'm going to ask but not right now" (because he was scared).

Well, Moran was older than they were and very bossy. She grabbed both of them by the arm, dragged them to their parent's bedroom door, and said, "Go ahead and ask them now."

Bustle was terrified not knowing what to expect because they just recently allowed her to have a boyfriend let alone get married. He knocked on the door, and they told him to come in. Bustle entered, but Money Mae stayed back by the door and did not enter. Bustle was nervous and with a trembling voice said, "Can I have your permission to marry your daughter, Money Mae?"

After he said that, the parents looked at each other. Her mom said, "What does Money Mae think about this?"

Bustle replied, "She said she wanted to marry me."

Her dad called her in the room and said, "Do you like this boy?"

The mom turned to her husband and said, "She's got to do more than just like him! If they're thinking about getting married, they have to know if they love each other."

She looked at Bustle and said, "Do you love Money Mae?"

Bustle replied, "Yes."

She then turned to Money Mae and said, "Well, do you love Bustle?"

Money Mae replied, "Yes."

The woman of God paused and then said, "Well, I guess you can get married then."

In just a short time, a month later, the two were married.

Chapter 14
Spiritual Growth

Bustle and Money Mae got married on 31 July 1982 and had a big wedding. They have five children: four boys and one girl. They prospered, and the Lord blessed them. Bustle continued studying the word of God and preached as the Lord led him. One of his powerful messages that the Lord had blessed him with was a message that he spoke on about courage. I'm going to give you that message verbatim. After the pastor had introduced him to the congregation, the members of the church all stood up clapping and praising God. Bustle stood up and walked toward the pulpit. He began to praise and thank and worship God along with the congregation for about 2 minutes.

As he did in almost all his messages, before he began, he testified, by saying, "Praise God! First of all, giving honor to God and to my pastor John Thompson, Praise God! Overseer in her absence. Praise God! All the deacons, Praise God! All the saints. I thank the Lord for being here. I thank the Lord for saving, sanctifying, and filling with the Holy Ghost!" It was then that he began to feel the spirit take over and began to speak with more authority and excitement.

He continued, "Thank the Lord for a mind to want to serve Him! Thank the Lord for His loving-kindness and tender mercy that He shed upon me! Praise God! God is a good God! God is a merciful God! God is a loving God! Praise God! And we, Praise God! Ought to praise His name because He's worthy of every praise! Praise God! The word of God is good! The word of God is life, health, and strength! Praise God! Not only to the spiritual man but to the physical man, Praise God! God is such a good God. I thank Him for His word, Praise God! We're blessed today; we're about to hear the word of God, Praise God! I'm going to sit back and let the Lord have His way, Praise God! Because it's His word! Hallelujah! As I began to study this lesson, Praise God! God began to bless me, began to bless me, began to bless me, Praise God! I am not going to tell you anything new. I am not going to tell you anything that you have not already heard. I'm not going to preach any Andre gospel to you because I DON'T HAVE ANY! Hallelujah!"

You could not only heard the excitement rising in Bustle's voice but also see and hear it in the congregation as well. They were echoing hallelujah, amen, and Praise God along with Bustle.

He continued, "I'm going to tell you about the word of God, Praise God! I'm going to bring back into remembrance to you the word of God. I want to let you know the importance of hearing God's word and being a doer of God's word. Praise God! The Lord is such a good God; He's such a good God; He loves each and every one of us; each and every one of us, He wants the best! Hallelujah! Not the

110

worst! Not the middle! He wants the besssst! Hallelujah! For us, Praise God!"

Now if you hadn't ever been to a Holy-Ghost-filled black church, you might think he was just yelling. But that wasn't the case. That's the way he was able to express himself through the spirit.

He continued, "We don't have to have our head hung down because God wants the best for us, Praise God! He doesn't want to whoop us and beat us down! He wants to encourage us and give us STRENGTH to be able to hold on to His word and do a work for Him! How can you do a work for Him when you BEAT DOWN? Hallelujah! Jesus! Jesus! Jesus! He wants to encourage us He wants to enable us with POWER! Hallelujah! To do His will to do His work, Praise God!

"Each and every one of us has a purpose; we have a duty we have something that God placed in us for us to do! DO YOU HEAR ME? Each and every one of us, from the littlest to the oldest, and God wants to be able to help us do the work for Him.

"All I want to do is give you a little bit of this word to encourage you, to enable you to do God's will and do His work, Praise God!"

He walked back to the pulpit and reached for his *Bible*, "Let's go to the book of Joshua starting at the first chapter the first verse. I'm only going to read nine verses, Praise God! I hope I'm going to be able to finish these nine because it's a lot just in these nine verses here! Praise God! Now, I'm going to read this. Now, although my main thing, the main topic that I'm going to be talking about his courage. But that covers a whole lot! This will cover a whole lot. I want you to focus on courage because God, He mentioned it in His word, but we're going to cover a whole lot here, Praise God! Praise the Lord!"

He had studied the word and was prepared for whichever way the Lord led him. Just like in any other profession when you get ready to do the most important part of your job, you wouldn't want anything to stand in your way. He knew that the message was going to get deep, and the emotions, or the spirit of the lord, were going to take us on a ride. So, he took off his jacket to be free and available for the Lord.

He explained, "I have to take off my jacket, Praise God! Because the word of God is good, Praise the Lord, Praise the Lord. I'm going to pray first:

Father God, In the name of Jesus, In the name of Jesus! We ask that your word go out forth and let it accomplish that it was set out to do. Lord use me as your vessel, Lord takes out everything that's not like you, In the name of Jesus! And let me be a vessel used by you, In the name of Jesus! And Lord let the word fall down in the good ground. Lord that they may Spring up and do a work for you. In the name of Jesus! In the name of Jesus! Lord let the words be in our hearts that we might not sin against you. In the name of Jesus! And we give your name the praise and all the glory and honor, belongs to you Lord, in Jesus name Amen, Praise God!

"I'm going to read these nine verses real quick, and it reads:

Now after the death of Moses the servant of the Lord it came to pass, that the Lord spake unto Joshua the son of Nun, Moses' minister, saying, Moses my servant is dead; now therefore arise, go over this Jordan, thou, and all this people, unto the land which I do give to them, even to the children of Israel. Every place that the sole of your foot shall tread upon, that have I given unto you, as I said onto Moses. From the wilderness and this Lebanon even unto the great River, the River Euphrates, all the land of the Hittites, and onto the great Sea towards the going down of the sun, shall be your coast. There shall not any man be able to stand before thee all the days of thy life: as I was with Moses, so I shall be with thee: I will not fail thee, nor forsake thee. Be strong and of a good courage: for onto this people shalt thou divide for an inheritance the land, which I sware onto their fathers to give them. Only be thou strong and very courageous, that thou mayest observe to do according to all the law, which Moses my servant commanded thee: turn not from it to the right hand or to the left, that thou mayest prosper whithersoever thou goest. This book of the law shall not depart out of thy mouth; but thou shalt meditate therein day and night, that thou mayest observe to do according to all that is written therein: for then thou shalt make thy way prosperous, and then thou shalt have good success. Have not I commanded thee? Be strong and of a good courage; be not afraid, neither be thou dismayed: for the Lord thy God is with thee whithersoever thou goest.

"Praise God! Just reading this word alone should enable you to go out and do God's will! And do God's mission! God loves us! He loves us! Praise God! Now, I'm going to break it down a little bit. Praise God! First of all, we're going to talk about courage. In order to do the work of God, you have to have some courage, matter-of-fact whenever you start to do anything! You're going to have to have some courage to do it! Jesus! Let's find out what courage is; let's find out the definition of courage. In the Webster's dictionary, courage is bravery; boldness; daring; fearless! Do you hear that! Bravery! You have to be brave! Because when you set out to do a work for God, it's all kinds of stuff that are going to stand in your way; of course, we heard about this in Sunday school. Praise God!

"You going to have to be brave; you're going to have to be bold, bold! You have to step out on God's word! Forget about what people say, bold! Step out, that's what courage is; you step out! God said that I will have life and that I'll have it more abundantly I'm going to have it! God said that He would forgive me of all my sins I've been forgiven! DO YOU HEAR WHAT I'M SAYING? That's what courage; that's what boldness is!

You step out on God's word; you don't care what people say, what they think, hallelujah! Just for you to understand, I am going to use an example of someone with courage; we can use a boxer. A boxer when he begins to train and getting ready, he believes that he can beat his opponent before he even steps in the ring with him because if you don't, he might as well sit down somewhere, what is he doing? What does he want to fight for? Why would he step in the ring for? If he didn't believe he could beat his opponent if you were scared and trembling."

Bustle stepped away from the pulpit and began to shake his body like someone that is scared, to demonstrate how ridiculous it would be for a boxer to act like before a fight.

He proceeded, "Hallelujah! Why step in the ring? A boxer has courage and boldness, fearless. Now that boldness, I'm going to give you the definition of boldness so you can understand what a Boxer has. The definition of boldness is presumption and presumption, is that may be assumed as true or valid until the contrary is proven! Do you hear what I'm saying? Look when a boxer steps in the ring, he says I'm going to win this fight! The only way I'm going to lose this fight is he is going to have to knock me out! Do you understand? You're going to have to fight for God, and the only way the devil is going to beat you is he has to knock you out. Do you understand what I'm saying?

"It says presumption is that may be assumed true or valid! When you believe God, you stand on His word! When you are courageous and have boldness, you know it to be fact; somebody is going to have to prove to me that it's not fact! Do you understand what I'm saying? Not because you said it's not fact, not because you said stop don't do what God says! That's not going to work! You've got to prove it to me!"

Bustle begins to get more emotional; you can hear it in his voice, the desperate plea to God, as he tries to hold back the tears while crying out the words that he speaks, listen. "God said He love me! God said He wants the best for me! Look! I'm not going to stop! I'm not going to give up! I'm going to believe His word until otherwise proven! Do you understand what I'm saying? That's what courage is, boldness, you stand on God's word; you believe He's going to do what He says. Jesus!

"The word of God is good, people! If you listen to this word of God, Praise God! You listen to the word of God, you will be blessed! You understand? That's all it takes to hear the word of God, and being a doer of His word, He will bless you. If you accept His word! If you accept His word and believe His word, that's the qualifications. Nicole Just read you're a new creature in him forget about the past His word says it, stand on His word. Jesus! Jesus! Okay now let's get off into the lesson."

Bustle began to read the first verse again and started to explain the relationship that Moses and God had (forward), "Now who was Moses? We know who Moses was; He delivered the children of Israel out of Egypt. Moses was a man that God knew face to face, it's in the word, Deuteronomy; 34:10."

Bustle walked back toward the pulpit to turn the pages of his *Bible* to that verse and read, "*And there arose not a prophet since in Israel like unto Moses, whom the Lord knew face to face.*"

He then looked up at the congregation and continued, "Now God knew Moses face-to-face. Now God is talking to Joshua; He's telling Joshua to take over where Moses left off and God knew Moses face-to-face. What I'm trying to say here is when we're doing a work for God, and He intends for us to do something He will enable us to do it. We don't have to say oh well I'm not so and so, I'm not Deacon Thompson; I'm not Deacon Smith; I'm not Minister Andre.

No, if God gives you a work to do, He'll bless you to do that. Praise the Lord!

"Now, Moses, we know even Moses when God gave Moses a work to do, he began to talk back a little bit and said Lord I can't even speak right. But Moses became so close to God, that God knows him face-to-face."

Bustle looked down at *The Bible* and read the second verse of Joshua the first chapter, "*Moses my servant is dead; now therefore arise, go over this Jordan, thou, and all this people, unto the land which I do give to them, even to the children of Israel.*"

Bustle began to expound on the word, "See, God gives us a mission, He gives us a charge, He gives us something to do! Praise God! Go to Judges; 6:14. Now, here's another man that God gave him something to do. I'm going to start at the 11th, verse."

Bustle went back to the pulpit and began to read, "*And there came an angel of the Lord, and sat under an oak which was in Ophrah, that pertained unto Joash the Abiezrite: and his son Gideon threshed wheat by the winepress, to hide it from the Midianites. And the angel of the Lord appeared unto him, and said unto him, The Lord is with thee, thou mighty man of valor. And Gideon said unto him, Oh, my Lord, if the Lord be with us, why then is all this befallen us? And where be all his miracles which our fathers told us of, saying, did not the Lord bring us up from Egypt? but now the Lord hath forsaken us, and delivered us into the hands of the Midianites.*"

Bustle looked at the congregation again and expounded on the word, "See, many of us say where is the Lord? If He's supposed to be by my side or with me, where is He?"

Bustle looked at his *Bible* and read the 14th, verse, "*And the Lord looked upon him, and said, Go, in this thy might, and thou shalt save Israel from the hand of the Midianites: have not I sent thee? And he said unto him, Oh, my Lord, wherewith shall I save Israel? Behold, my family is poor in Manasseh, and I am the least in my father's house.*"

Bustle stopped at the end of the 15th, verse and began to expound on the word, "See we don't have an excuse if we say I don't have nothing. I don't have anything to offer. Gideon said my family is poor, and I am the least in the house of these poor people, see God can use you no matter what situation you're in, you can't say, well, I've kind of been going astray for so long, so many years I haven't been doing God's will anyway, so I might as well cruise down the same highway.

"No, no, God has a work for you to do and it doesn't matter the situation that's going on right now. Do you understand what I'm trying to say? Gideon said my household is poor! Do you hear what I'm saying? And I am the least in the house of these poor people, if God can use that poor man, He can use us. When God has a work for you to do God will enable you to do that work. What I'm doing, as I said, I'm just trying to break it down to you.

"God loves us; He doesn't want us to be in poverty; He doesn't want that; God doesn't want that! He wants blessings for us, see He's talking to Joshua and you know the children of Israel, I just got to tell it, see, I've been reading this word of God and the children of Israel, they were just rebellious; rebellious, rebellious, rebellious. God had done so many things, so many works, yet and still, they still served idle gods."

Bustle began to walk back and forth then with more emotion said, "But God loved them! He loved the children of Israel! He sent prophet after prophet to deliver them out of the hands of their enemies. God is a good God, what I'm trying to tell you people is that you don't have to look down, God will bless you right now. Do you hear what I'm saying! It doesn't matter what situation you're in, God will bless you, just be courageous! So, God gave Joshua a mission."

Bustle walked back to the pulpit and began to read the 3rd and 4th verses, *"Every place that the soul of your foot shall tread upon, that have I given unto you, as I said unto Moses. From the wilderness and this Lebanon even onto the great river, the river Euphrates, all the land of the Hittites, and onto the great sea toward the going down of the sun, shall be your coast."*

Bustle then looked up, stepped away from the pulpit, and expounded on the word of God. "God will bless you with the best, for example, what I get out of this, that I am reading here if I apply this to modern days, we know that beachfront property is the best, it's expensive. You see what I'm saying! He said that every place that the sole of your foot shall tread upon, where ever you go! And you step on this! And say I want that! God will bless you with it! Jesus! Praise God! God will bless us but we have to be, what?"

Bustle paused to receive the answer from the congregation, then repeated, "We have to be, what?"

Then the congregation replied, "Courageous!"

Then Bustle continued, "Courageous! See all of this goes together, we can't say I want the good of the land, I want the wine and you know, all the good of land but don't step out to get it and be courageous, you're not going to get it. See God emphasized it so much that He kept repeating it, He said but be courageous, He said to be strong and very courageous. Now after He said it, He said haven't I commanded you to be strong! Jesus! Jesus!"

Bustle walked back to the pulpit and began to read the fifth verse with great emotion. "*There shall not any*! Any! Any! Any! There should not any! Any! Any! *Man be able to stand before thee all the days of thy life.*"

Bustle stopped reading and expounded on the word, "See you'll be invincible! It says there will be no man able to stand before you, but the key is you have to have God with you because He said that He will be with you, the word says that there shall not be any man able to stand before you all the days of your life; as I was with Moses, so I will be with thee. See Moses was able to do all of those miracles because God was with him! Do you understand what I'm saying?

"Now you can be courageous all you want, but if you ain't got God and He's not with you, you'll fall every time, see you have to have, just like our pastor said you have to eat the whole roll. You got to have all of this word, you can't take bits and pieces of *The Bible* and say, I'm going to abide by this! I'm going to abide by that! Then expected it to work! You have to take all of the words. Hallelujah! You want the blessings of the Lord you're going to have to stand on His word and be courageous! And have God in your life, this is how you can be blessed. Jesus!

"*I will not fail thee, nor forsake thee*. Divine presence! He will always be with you. He said I will never fail you nor forsake you, never forsake you, Divine custody! He will always be your father, He won't give you up, He won't leave you abandoned! Do you hear what I'm saying? In front of somebody's doorstep, for someone else to take care of you. He will be there always, if He's your Lord, He'll be there always."

Bustle walked back to the pulpit and read 6th verse, "*Be strong and of good courage: for unto this people shalt thou divide for an inheritance the lane, which I sware onto their fathers to give them.* Be strong, be strong, that being strong is not talking about having some muscle."

Bustle began to curl his arm to make a muscle in his biceps and pointed at it to illustrate it not meaning, necessarily to have physical strength. "Be strong, hold on, hold on to God, be strong, don't wither, don't be weary, be strong in him, be strong and of good courage. Praise God! I'm going to talk about being strong, a little bit."

Bustle walked back over to the pulpit and told the congregation to turn their *Bibles* to II Chronicles; 15:7.

Then someone out of the congregation started reading that verse. "*Be strong therefore, and let not your hands be weak: for your work shall be rewarded.*"

Then Bustle expounded on the word. "See if you hold on and be strong in the Lord, you will be rewarded. Go to II Timothy; 2:4."

As Bustle turned his *Bible* to find that verse, someone else in the congregation found it and started reading, "*No man that warreth entangleth himself with the affairs of this life; that he may please him who hath chosen him to be a soldier.*"

Bustle started expounding on the word once more, "If you are in a warfare, you're going to have to be strong and you cannot entangle yourself with the cares of this world. Praise God! Go to Joshua; 21: 43."

Bustle went to his *Bible* and found that verse and started reading from it, "*And the Lord gave onto Israel all the land which he sware to give onto their fathers; and they possessed it, and dwelt therein. And the Lord gave them rest round about, according to all that he sware onto their fathers: and their stood not a man of all their enemies before them; the Lord delivered all their enemies onto their hand there failed not ought of any good thing which the Lord had spoken unto the house of Israel; all came to pass.*

"Everything that God said it came to pass. God didn't just say it He performed it! It said that there failed not ought of any good thing which the Lord had spoken onto the house of Israel; all came to pass! All came to pass! God will bless you if you hold on. Let's go back to Joshua; 1:7."

Bustle started looking at his *Bible* and turned the pages back to that verse and read, "*Only be strong and very courageous, that thou mayest observed to do according to all the law, which Moses my servant commanded thee: turn not from it to the right-hand or to the left, that thou mayest prosper whithersoever thou goest.*"

Bustle started expounding on the word, "See doing God's will, will only bring prosperity. Doing His will, will only bring prosperity, but we can't turn to the right or the left, we have to do His will, we have to be courageous and do His will and God will do everything He said He would do."

Bustle continued reading, "*This book of the law shall not depart out of thy mouth; but thou shalt meditate therein day and night, that thou mayest observe to do according to all that is written therein: for then* (see only after you have obeyed His will then) *thou shalt make thy way prosperous, and then thou shalt have good success* (after you do His will and listen to His word)."

Bustle continued with the 9th verse, "Have not I commanded thee to be strong and of good courage. See you have to have the courage to obtain this, so it's good to have good things, but you are going to have to go through and do it with some courage.

"Praise God! The word of God is good. I just want to give you one more verse, II Chronicles; 16:9 Praise the Lord! Now listen, I read this verse here, and I was blessed. I was really blessed with this verse.

"Now the word of God says, the devil goes to and fro seeking who he made defile.

"That's the devil's job, that's what he does. He goes to and fro seeking who he may defile, that's what he's doing, he's doing it right now. Hallelujah! Hallelujah!

"Hallelujah! Oooooh! But we got a God! We got a God!"

Bustle began to speak with even more emotion and continued, "We got a God! We got a God! The word hear says, for the eyes of the Lord run to and fro throughout the whole earth. Do you hear me! The devil may be going out to seek who he may defile, but God is right there, to show Himself strong on behalf of them whose heart is perfect toward Him!

"Now listen, God is a good God, you don't have to wary about what the devil is doing, God is right there if you let the Lord in your heart, He'll work in you, the devil ain't got time to come and defile you. The word said the devil goes

123

to and fro seeking who he may defile. But the eyes of the Lord run to and fro throughout the whole Earth. Nobody was left out! Do you hear me! Nobody was left out. Do you hear what I'm saying!

"He's looking for a vessel; He's looking for somebody willing to be used by Him. To and fro throughout the whole Earth, God has no respective person. Did you hear what Gideon said, I'm poor, my whole household is poor, and I am the least in the house, what does God have to do with somebody like me how can I deliver Israel! Do you hear what I'm saying! But the Lord is looking for somebody, to show Himself strong in, on your behalf. Do you hear what I'm saying!

"He wants good things to happen, to you! He wants blessings to happen to you! He wants you to be set free! He wants you to be delivered! He wants you to go out and do a work for Him, it's on your behalf. Not that things may go wrong for you, but things work out for you on your behalf. God is a good God! He's a merciful God! He's a looooooooooving God! Hallelujah!"

Bustle started leaving the pulpit area and walked down toward the middle of the alter, to get close to the congregation, and continued speaking, "He loves each and every one of us, our God is working for us on our behalf, He's working for us. He's such a good God, why wouldn't you want to serve a God like this? He wants blessing for us, He wants us to be prosperous and have good success. He said but be ye strong and of good courage."

God is such a good God, that's why I praise Him, that's why I praise Him because He's such a good God. I've been blessed I've been blessed by the Lord. I'm not going to say that I'm filthy rich, or anything like that, but God has blessed me. You know what? I didn't graduate from High School. I don't have a High School Diploma and I stop going to school in about the 10th or 11th grade. I was enrolled in school I may have been enrolled in school but I wasn't going. Praise God! I was illiterate! Do you hear me? I couldn't read a lick.

God is a good God. He's a merciful God. The Lord has blessed me, it's His blessings Praise the Lord! I have a house; it's a big house I didn't think that I was going to be able to afford it. But He blessed me with this big house and I was able to put a pool in the backyard, God blessed me with that. Praise God! He blessed me to fix it up like I wanted to fix it up. Praise God!

God bless me with this, a matter of fact my wife the other day came to me because you know, she does the books. After so many years, I turn the books over to her and she said, 'I don't know how we're going to pay for this or how we're going to pay for that,' and I said, 'Don't worry about it, don't worry.' First of all, my joy is in the Lord! Not in those things Do you hear what I'm saying?

"For I know God is able to bless me, to keep those things, if I put my trust in Him. Praise God! And if I'm not able to keep those things or lose them whatever the case may be, I have Joy in the Lord! Do you understand me! But God is such a God, He says, 'You love me and I love you, I can't see you walking around here with nothing, what kind of father would be if I did that?' I'm a father, and I don't want to see my boys walking around here with nothing! Do you hear what I'm saying! Sometimes, I reach in my pocket, (for my money) and don't get the stuff that I want from me (but let me leave it in my pocket) so that my boys may have it. God loves us more than I love my own children, He loves us so, that He wants the best for us! Do you understand me!

"He wants us to prosper, that's how much He loves. Praise God! Even the finance people, we were looking to refinance and we gave them our information and stuff, and the finance lady said, 'I can't understand how you guys are able to pay your bills, with the income that you guys say you have and all the stuff that you have, how are you making it month-to-month?' The Lord is blessing us, that's how good God is! Praise God!

"I think God for His word, I just want you to realize how much God loves you, I just want you to realize how much He loves you! He wants the best for you and if you take the word of God in your heart and you let it fall down on that good ground, it's going to, spring up. But if you leave it by the wayside, or you keep things entangled in your life and planet it in the thorns or you don't get it deep down in you, it's going to burnout. Let the word of God go on the good ground because He loves us, He loves us! He wants us to prosper Praise God!"

My Beginnings

Pookie, Bustle, and Heavy

Bustle's Gunshot Wounds

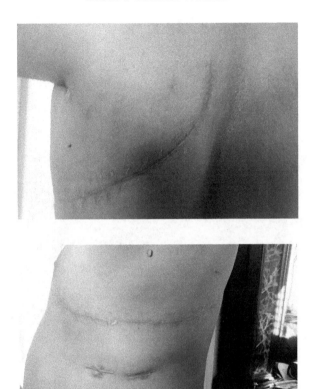

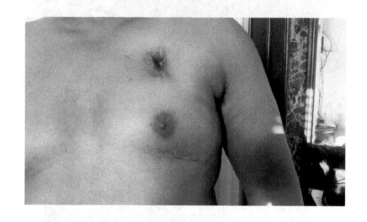

Walking Miracle

Bustle and Money Mae's Wedding Day

And Their Children

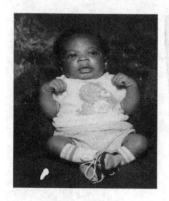

Andre Junior, Lvan, Andrea, Samuel, and Timothy

God Answers Prayers. He Got More than Just One Child.

CPSIA information can be obtained
at www.ICGtesting.com
Printed in the USA
LVHW022129010921
696650LV00010B/640